God Wants You to Smile

EILEEN GUDER

God Wants You to Smile

Doubleday & Company, Inc., Garden City,
New York 1974

ISBN: 0-385-03521-7
Library of Congress Catalog Card Number 73–11706

BY THE SAME AUTHOR

What Happened After
We're Never Alone
To Live in Love
Living in Both Worlds
The Many Faces of Friendship
The Naked I
God, But I'm Bored!

CONTENTS

CHAPTER ONE
There's a Little Blue in Everyone's Color Scheme   1

   YOU'RE NOT ALONE   3
   GENESIS AND HOW WE GOT HERE   6
   OUT OF HARMONY   9
   DOWN BUT NOT OUT   12

CHAPTER TWO
The Lighter Shades of Blue   15

   WHAT'S YOUR PROBLEM?   16
   THE COMPULSIVE WORKER   19
   KEEP IT IN PROPORTION   21
   ADMIT THE BLUES EXIST   24
   THE BIG AND THE LITTLE   25
   GETTING ORGANIZED   29

CHAPTER THREE
Patches of Blue   33

   DEFEATING HOUSEWORK   33
   THE FRAZZLE OF FINANCES   36
   NOBODY'S PERFECT   39
   IT'S UP TO YOU   42

CONTENTS

CHAPTER FOUR

How Did I Get This Way?   45

FREEDOM OF CHOICE   46
THE PROBLEM OF TEMPERAMENT   48
IT'S YOUR DECISION   50
"REAP A CHARACTER"   52

CHAPTER FIVE

The Hidden Adversary   57

ACCEPT YOURSELF   57
THE QUEST FOR PERFECTION   60
THE BAD AND THE GOOD   62
SO WHY NOT CHANGE?   64
A PERSONAL EXPERIENCE   67
AND VICTORY   71

CHAPTER SIX

Trapped in a Molasses Vat   75

A FRIEND'S STORY   76
THE RESULTS   79
"HOPELESS" CIRCUMSTANCES   81
IMPOSSIBLE PEOPLE   84
THE HIGHEST CHRISTIAN LOVE   87
THE LIMPET AND WHAT TO DO   91
THE CLINGING YOU   95

CHAPTER SEVEN

They'll Be Sorry   99

MASK FOR ANGER   99
WHOSE FAULT?   101
THE VICIOUS CYCLE   103
THE FALLACY OF "VICTORIOUS" CHRISTIANS   106

Contents

CHAPTER EIGHT
Ghosts in the House   113

FEAR OF FAILURE   115
PEOPLE AND LONELINESS   117
TALK TO GOD   120
KEEP GOING   123

CHAPTER NINE
Don't Look, It May Go Away   127

BEYOND OUR CONTROL   128
THE DEVIL VS. THE HOLY SPIRIT   129
THE DEEPER REALITY   134
LEAVING YOUTH BEHIND   136
BE HAPPY IN YOUR AGE   138

CHAPTER TEN
Is There a Magic Key?   141

THE SOURCE OF THE PROBLEM   143
CHARACTER AND WHAT IT IS   144
YOU CAN CHANGE   146
GOD, THE BIBLE AND YOU   149

God Wants You to Smile

CHAPTER ONE

There's a Little Blue in Everyone's Color Scheme

The decision to write a book about the blues and what can be done to get rid of them came primarily as a result of my own experience. It was confirmed innumerable times by conversations like this:

"What are you working on now, Eileen?"

"I'm doing a book on the blues."

"You are! Oh, I wish you'd written it three years ago when I *really* went through a terrible low . . ." or, "Let me tell you about my sister, she . . ." or, "When will it be out? My mother is driving me right up the wall, and maybe a book like this will help her."

However, writing a book about the blues or, if you want to be a little more tony, depression, can be a risky business. In the first place many readers will immediately expect a psychologist's handbook for the layman, abounding in such terms as *regressive, traumatic, anxiety level* and *introject.* Or if not that, then another of the multitudinous books written in the first person and telling all about the writer's own bouts with depression or alcoholism or mental illness, complete with lurid descriptions.

1

Both kinds of book have value, but seem to me to be somewhat limited for most of us. If we take the psychological approach we must study psychology to some degree or be content with only a partial understanding of the book. Even the terms used must be read with a dictionary in one hand and the book in the other. But what is there for the person who doesn't want a layman's course in psychology, who wants merely to handle the occasional fit of the blues a little bit better?

As for the "I've been through it" approach, some people, myself among them, are so impressionable that reading the book is like a trip through the local asylum —profoundly depressing in itself. Again, these books speak of extremes, even if we find them interesting rather than horrifying, and are beside the point—a little like being presented an explanation of calculus when all you wanted to know was how to balance your check record.

Besides, there already are more than enough books in both categories. This one, therefore, is for the person plagued by occasional attacks of the blues that make one miserable but do not yet incapacitate. There will be some psychological terms in it, of course, because we live in that kind of world. We all are so much surrounded by the terms, attitudes, thoughts and beliefs of the various schools of psychology that we can't avoid them. We pick them up by osmosis.

It will include personal experiences, too; we are writing about an intensely personal subject. Although this is not, as I have already said, a biography of my own or anyone else's traumas, it would not be fair to leave out personal experience entirely. To some extent, one must be personal to be honest. I'd rather say, "it seems to me," or, "this has worked in my own life and I've seen it work for others," than to claim omnipotence. I'm always distrustful of the proposition contained in a sentence that begins, "It is well known that," or, "No one disputes the fact that," because all too often the asserted universal acceptance does not, in fact, exist.

And, of course, everyone loves a story. We are a pragmatic people, and we don't really accept a proposition or theory unless we see it demonstrated. We want to know what happens to people more than what conclusions a line of argument leads to. Beliefs, whether they are about God or the reliability of banks or a friend's word, have to be demonstrated to be credible. We easily affirm the truth of all sorts of propositions we have no intention of ever testing because they do not impinge on our lives at all. But when it comes to matters we encounter every day— our relationships with others, the problems of acceptance and achievement and happiness—we want to *know:* Does this idea work for others, and if so, how?

YOU'RE NOT ALONE

If neither psychology nor personal experience is the basis for the book, though both may figure in it to some degree, that does not mean there isn't a cohesive view of life at the bottom of it. There is. I'm writing from the point of view of one who believes that God made me as well as the world and that He cares about me and my world. I'm not in this alone, an insignificant little blob in the universe trying to work out some meaning before I vanish. I'm important because God created me and has a plan for me. There is a goal worth all our bruises and scars. What we need to know is how to handle our manner of getting there so as to eliminate all the unnecessary knocks.

This is not to say I believe in the milk-and-water type of Christianity that views God as a sort of heavenly stage manager who will, if approached correctly, shift things around constantly so as to remove all possible sources of harm from our proximity. That *is* a currently popular view, but neither the world as it is nor the Bible bears it out. There are some wounds we sustain just by being here. We are surrounded by all sorts of people, and their actions make a difference in our lives, just as what we do affects others. Events beyond our control—massive changes in world politics for instance—alter not only the world scene but our own lives. Today's grocery bill is higher than last year's for many reasons, some of them as far away as southeast Asia, Japan or Paris.

There is a sense in which it is easy enough to accept all that, to understand that although human beings are responsible for most of the troubles around, God is working out His purpose and eventually all the wrong, sad, debilitating situations in life will be put right. I know Christians who can bear all sorts of calamities with genuine fortitude; they know that life is full of risks and possible wounds and can face them with serenity. They are, after all, living in a world that is, for the most part, operating as if God did not exist and in a manner certainly not to His liking. The life of a Christian is frequently made a lot more difficult when he tries to live according to God's wishes in such a world. He's bound to get hurt.

But even many of these people, serene enough in the face of the blows we all sustain from time to time, become upset and petulant when they can't cope with problems that seem to come from within. After all, they reason, we are not responsible for what other people do to us. There may even be a kind of self-conscious glow of virtue about being brave and un-complaining in the face of troubles. One can always give a testimony about it, telling how God has given grace to go through the whole mess with courage, and the comfortable conviction that one is speaking with humility and even a bit of humor and demonstrating all the Christian virtues does a lot to assuage the trouble. It's nice to be a hero, even if it's in a small way.

But depression, that sinking feeling which creeps up when we're not expecting it, turns the world to gray. There's nothing spiritual about it, we can't put our finger on the cause, and why—*why* should this happen to me? There are certain biblical teachings about some of the causes of the blues, which will be considered later.

5

However, as far as I can tell there is no hint in the entire Bible that being a Christian exempts one from whatever risks being alive in this world entails. We walk on the same streets as everyone else, we eat the same food, drink the same drinks, must cope with the same economy and are certainly exposed to the same diseases. We are also prone to the same emotional ups and downs.

GENESIS AND HOW WE GOT HERE

The basic premise of the Bible, which I—along with countless others in the past two thousand years—believe to be true, is based on the first three chapters of Genesis, and is absolutely fundamental to everything that follows—in the Bible and in human history. If you want to know why we're in the mess we're in, you must discover how we got here, which is exactly what that story tells us. Let me give you my free translation.

You will remember that when God made the earth, He capped the whole job by creating man. Man was the crowning achievement, and he was put in charge, so to speak. He had a job to do. "Be fruitful and multiply, and fill the earth and subdue it; and have dominion over the fish of the sea and over the birds of the air and over every living thing that moves upon the earth."

The second chapter of Genesis tells the whole story over again, adding some details. Adam and Eve were put in the Garden of Eden and the description indi-

6

cates that God provided everything they needed—not only food, but beauty. Eden was lovely—it had "every tree that is pleasant to the sight and good for food . . ." The aesthetic side of man was taken care of.

In the middle of the garden was the tree of life and the tree of the knowledge of good and evil. Adam and Eve were told by God that they could eat freely of everything *except* the tree of the knowledge of good and evil, for if they ate it they would die. God had paid His own creatures the honor of giving them a will and freedom in which to operate. They could make a choice.

Eve met a stranger in the garden one day and he said something like this to her:

"Well, nice little place you have here—looks very pleasant. The Lord seems to have done very well by you. But is it all yours?"

Eve said, "Of course it's ours! Why, we're in charge of the whole place. We run it—under the Lord's direction, of course—but we *do* run it. Oh—that one tree, right there in the middle—the Lord did tell us not to eat of it—indeed, not even touch it, lest we die."

At that the serpent said, "Why, you won't die at all! You poor thing, that tree is the best thing in the whole place—I don't know how you can run things properly without it as it will give you knowledge of good and evil. God ought not to keep *that* back from you—could be jealousy, of course, for if you do eat it, you'll be like He is, knowing good and evil. I think you owe

7

it to yourself to try it—to fulfill your potential as a woman."

Of course the silly thing fell for it and ate, and so did Adam. It's at this point that so many odd misconceptions about sin have crept into the story. Some people have thought the sin had something to do with sex, since Adam and Eve were naked until they ate the fruit and then—the story tells us—realized for the first time that they were naked and scurried around to get some clothes on.

The meaning of the story is far profounder than that, and its implications go far deeper. They believed a slander about God—and in believing that lie they began to distrust Him. The serpent implied to them that some good thing, something necessary to them, was being held back by God. He wasn't taking care of them. They would have to look out for themselves. They might even be better off, since this new knowledge would make them like God, and for the first time they not only distrusted Him but felt competitive toward Him. Theologians say that pride is the basic sin, and the essence of that pride was a desire to compete with God. No wonder the relationship was broken! It wasn't that God, like an oriental despot, threw them out the first time they flouted Him, but that their distrust of Him—their refusal to believe Him, really, since everything the serpent said was a flat contradiction of what He told them—made a clear relationship impossible.

Of course, two things immediately happened when

8

they ate the fruit. They *did* have the knowledge of good and evil; but it was a sad knowledge that they themselves were not right—no longer able to stand before God. They saw their own nakedness and it was, I believe, more than a physical nakedness—it was all their own inadequacy not only to face God honestly but to face each other. The loss of trust in God had done something irreparable. It had made it impossible to ever totally trust one another again.

What God had warned them would happen also took place. They died. Oh, not physically—not then. That came later. But the certain something God had put within them at creation so that He could say of His handiwork that it was very good—that was gone. Theologians call it righteousness. Whatever we call it, it was gone. They were—and we all are—flawed creatures, incapable of doing what we know to be right, so that however hard we try and with whatever good intentions the result is always a little warped.

There were other consequences. Adam and Eve could no longer accept the love of God freely, as they had. They hid from Him and He was obliged to seek them out. In a sense everything that has happened since that time is the story of His seeking us out. The rest of the Bible is the story of God's reaching out to man in one way or another until it culminates in the person of Jesus Christ.

OUT OF HARMONY

We not only hide ourselves away from Him but from each other. In losing our ability to be loved by God, we can no longer love each other without encumbrance. Human love is probably the most sought after, praised, longed-for commodity there is, but it's also the greatest problem.

In addition to losing their original rightness and their ability to receive God's love, their sense of identity became blurred. They had known who they were because God had told them. He not only told them who they were in relationship to Himself and to each other, but gave them a job—a function. They were to be in charge of the earth and all its creatures. One can see the order in everything at that point. Men in obedience to God, obedience lived out in a clear, unbroken relationship with Him, that certain something inside them that was "just right" enabling them to do by nature what we find impossible or highly difficult—be good people. Their lives together pervaded by the same harmony, and the animal world ruled by them without exploitation.

All that was changed. No longer Eden, a lovely garden, but dust and thorns and thistles and enmity between man and beast. Everything, in short, was thrown out of kilter when Adam and Eve were out of harmony with God.

They left the garden. Though the record does not say so, I have in my mind a very clear picture of the two of them sitting down just the other side of the door as it clanged shut behind them. They made out two sets of rules—Adam made out a set for Eve, and she made out a set for him. We have been making rules ever since, most of them with other people in mind. Life is very difficult when you don't have a clear sense of identity and cannot love or be loved as you would like to, not to mention our inability to behave as we should.

No wonder we're depressed at times! We have reason to be. We're always just a little out of sync, as it were. Even Christians. This is very hard for some people to accept. They have come to believe that being a Christian means that all our wrongness is put right, and therefore life will be uncomplicated, a mere matter of following Christ's set of rules instead of whatever we lived by before.

It's not that simple. In the first place, Christ didn't give us rules—He gave us guidelines or principles. Making them work in our everyday situations is at times problematical because of the ambiguous world in which we live. There are times when to do what we know we should will cost us money or friends—or entree into certain circles—and other times when it's difficult to decide just what *is* the right thing to do.

Even if we always knew what to do (as some uncomplicated people assume), we are not yet perfect and either haven't the will or the desire to do the right thing. All our emotions, habits of thinking and reacting are holdovers from life apart from Christ and have to be changed so as to enable us to fit into His kingdom. That change is gradual, spasmodic and at times delayed by our own reluctance to be altered in any way.

You can see how, given a crazy mixed-up world and an imperfect set of emotions and character traits, we aren't going to be automatically good and wise because we are Christians. One of the results of both the external circumstances that constantly bewilder and frustrate us and our own inner conflicts will be, from time to time, a fit of the blues. Sometimes it will be temporary and fairly light; other times it will go so deep as to deserve to be called a depression. It may even become pathological and, given certain temperaments on which to work, so crippling that professional help is called for.

DOWN BUT NOT OUT

There *is* a time to run for the doctor. When one is so depressed that to function normally is impossible, or when the depression alternates with wild swings into unreasoning exhilaration, or when the depression becomes suicidal it is utter folly not to get the best professional counselor possible. There's nothing disgraceful in having an emotional problem, though a shallow, pseudo-Christian philosophy says so—as if becoming a Christian were a sort of spiritual vitamin pill which made all illness impossible.

Sometimes we bring into our Christian experience so many hangovers from the old life that we can't even grasp all we need to know to function as Christians. Then help is called for. A psychologist, Dr. Raymond Cramer, used to say, "If you take a sick person and impose a Christian experience on him, you get a sick

12

There's a Little Blue in Everyone's Color Scheme

Christian." That person's spiritual standing may be fine, but his emotional health needs more than Bible verses in order to be whole.

However, most of us live somewhere in the middle of the emotional scale, neither always on top nor under it so far we can't operate. We get along pretty well, have our times of robust health, emotionally speaking, and the occasional lows which we would like very much to handle—somehow—better than we do now.

The Church was meant to be a community of believers living in a harmonious relationship with each other; the family of God, where we can be ourselves and find mutual strength and encouragement. We have a tendency to think of the church as a specific building and the particular group of people holding membership in its rolls. That is not the biblical view. The Church is the whole body of believers and whatever individual church one belongs to is simply a little bit of the whole. That specific group, or family, though a part of the larger family, ought to be the place where each member of it finds what he needs to keep going in life, just the way members of an individual family come together for rest and food and relaxation from the day's work.

Paul wrote to the Christians at Ephesus reminding them that they were one body. He also remarked in a discussion of the life of a believer, that "we are not separate units but intimately related to each other in Christ." In the same vein he advised the Thessalonians this way: "Live together in peace, and our in-

13

struction to this end is to reprimand the unruly, encourage the timid, help the weak and be very patient with all men." That is a good description of what goes on in a human family.

We can encourage one another—most of us need more than anything else just to know someone is for us. It puts new heart into us. A sympathetic (though certainly not sentimental) friend can do wonders when one is a little low in spirits.

In that sense friends who share the same viewpoint, as Christians were meant to, can be the greatest lift to anyone suffering from the blues. It was necessary to say, "were meant to," because unfortunately Christians do not always share the same viewpoint and they are not always encouraging and helpful. By sharing the same viewpoint I do not mean agreeing on every issue, but that we have a common allegiance to Christ and His purposes in the world and in our lives. We all use the available resources of this world to keep our balance—doctors, psychologists, marriage counselors, financial advisers, bankers, lawyers—but we are not limited to these. We have been promised help from beyond, spiritual resources for the most gruelling tests of endurance. Again, Paul described our situation most aptly. (He was such a passionate human being; angry, joyous, hurt at times, discouraged, stubborn, loving— the antithesis of the bloodlessly placid saint so often depicted as a Christian ideal.) "We may be knocked down," he wrote the troublesome church at Corinth, "but we are never knocked out!"

14

CHAPTER TWO

The Lighter Shades of Blue

A sense of proportion is a major necessity for living a balanced life. Without it one cannot cope with the changing moods we all experience, and we are all liable to feel just a little bit blue from time to time. Who hasn't gotten up some mornings with a vague sense of depression? The day yawns ahead, full of unpalatable obligations—dishes to be done, housework awaits just as it does every morning; the luncheon date with a friend suddenly excites no interest. Life is just flat.

Most of us get through these gray days the best way we can knowing that the mood will pass. There are those, however, unprepared for the low times, totally disorganized by them and at the mercy of the mood. One friend of mine seemed never to realize that the moods she felt would go away, just as they had gone away before. She reacted to every day's emotional temperature as if it were the first time she had ever felt that way, and it might last forever.

"Oh, Eileen," she would exclaim as I opened the front door, "I'm so depressed. I woke this morning just *knowing* that it will never work out." ("It" was always whatever current love affair or new job or vacation plan was her main interest.) She never seemed able to remember from one time to the next that her mood, whatever its cause, would pass; the situation that seemed so hopeless would, as before, even out and the crisis shrink to manageable size. She had no sense of proportion.

I remember laughing years ago when a woman told me she was troubled by a nervous itch that came upon her at times of stress. She would sit and scratch her arms, the itch making her frustration even worse. Finally, her husband said, "Abbie, I do wish you'd try to save your itching for really serious problems! Don't just itch for everything that comes along, keep it for the big troubles."

You can't always stop itching on demand, but you can do something about the mental itch that develops into the blues. These minor irritations in life are not going to disappear; there is no recipe for a life free of troubles, either big or little. They are always with us, like the common cold, and like it attack the just and the unjust alike. We can't get rid of them, but we can minimize them.

WHAT'S YOUR PROBLEM?

The first thing is to identify the particular gremlin lurking behind whatever blue mood or depression one has. There's something vaguely frightening about being emotionally low for no apparent reason. No doubt

16

we have all been so conditioned by the superabundance of articles and books on psychology that the slightest change in our feelings causes the mind to leap to such terms as, "manic-depressive," "psychotic," "neurotic," and the rest of them. We live in a culture that is highly subjective, encouraging us to examine ourselves minutely for the slightest deviation from the normal. Whatever that is.

Like any other tool men use, psychology can be used wrongly; my own personal conviction is that when anyone becomes so obsessed with himself that he is constantly analyzing and probing his own interior to see what makes him tick, he's using the tool in a foolish and dangerous manner. When I wrote that one identifies the cause of a slight feeling of the blues, I did *not* mean the kind of intensive self-analysis we associate with psychologists and psychiatrists. I meant simply to stop and think about the present conditions that could be the cause of the blues. Not whether your mother rejected you or not, but do you have a cold?

Or have you been overworking or not getting enough sleep or having your in-laws as house guests. There are all kinds of ordinary situations that can and often do produce a temporary feeling of depression. Once those causes are recognized, the vague, formless alarm we feel at not being in top form is gone. There's a reason for being under it, and sometimes the reason is so overwhelming that it would be absolutely inhuman not to be a little bit blue.

Then, of course, one is faced with the question of the

cure. If it's merely not enough sleep, there's a remedy for that. If it's overwork, that's usually spasmodic and there's relief in sight. If it's a cold, there's always the knowledge that sooner or later the Kleenex and the cold pills will have had their day. It too will pass.

The most important thing is not to act on the basis of the mood. That's where a sense of proportion is the major aid to getting over the blues. It enables one to say, "Yes, I'm certainly low today, and why not? The kids are home from school with colds, the washing machine is broken and we're not making our food budget this month. But I know this won't last forever. They *will* go back to school tomorrow, even if today seems like eternity. The mechanic will be here this afternoon to fix the washer, and we've survived these minor financial crises before. We will again. Rather than let myself get hysterical because suddenly life's all wrong, I think I'll shut the bedroom door on my darling children, fix myself a cup of hot tea and put my feet up for half an hour while I read the mystery novel I got from the library."

You see, a sense of proportion tells us that small irritations need small remedies. No need to bring out the surgical knives when the trouble is, so to speak, nothing but a pimple. It's at this point that too many people miss the boat. They usually do it for one of three reasons.

First, they may have been brought up to be compulsive workers, feeling guilty if they're not achieving something every minute so that the idea of an afternoon lazed away in reading a mystery novel seems almost like sacrilege. They may, like my temperamental friend, have never learned to tell the difference between a small frustration and a major disaster, so that life is one trauma after another. Or they may be the product of a Christian point of view that teaches that the really "spiritual" Christian does not have these ups and downs. He leads the "victorious" Christian life, which is taken to mean that nothing, from a bee sting to sudden death in the family, will ever shake his serenity. This last point of view is the deadliest menace and the most difficult to eradicate because those who suffer—and they do suffer—in its grip really believe that their very faith would disappear if they did not hold on to this erroneous point of view.

THE COMPULSIVE WORKER

But first—the compulsive worker, who feels guilty if she isn't accomplishing some worthwhile goal every minute of the day. She gets uptight, she gets depressed and frustrated, but because she is compelled to achieve in order to feel she has a right to be alive she just goes grimly through the blues. The pain she suffers is no worse than the pain she inflicts on those around her, if as much. Since she must constantly be busy, others must be too. The idea that one can be usefully employed just in thinking without moving a muscle, is incomprehensible to her. Still worse, the thought of going out for an afternoon's shopping without any particular goal in mind—just out. She requires of her family the same devotion to duty that she gives, whether the duties are worth it or not.

It would do no good to tell such a woman that life is more than getting the housework done, or the children educated or a bank account up to twenty thousand dollars because she wouldn't believe it. She must just suffer her blue periods until she is willing to discover that achieving isn't everything. Usually this happens only in a most catastrophic manner. The husband she's too busy for finds a woman who has time to play; the children grow up and leave home and come back reluctantly and as seldom as possible. An illness comes and suddenly cuts all her busyness short. These are intensely painful experiences, and sometimes when they are over a better perspective is gained. But at what a cost!

If you are this kind of woman, there isn't much I can say here that will convince you it's all right not to be engaged in some project every moment except that just doing nothing isn't necessarily being lazy, and sometimes it's the quickest way out of a depression caused by too much work, too much pressure. Changing your outlook won't be easy—but if you are not willing to try, you will have to cope with your own particular demons of depression the best way you can.

But if you are the child or wife or husband of this woman, there is something you can do. It sounds brutal, but it is really the kindest, most constructive action you can take. Don't let her bully you into following her life pattern. Be kind, be gentle, if possible, but be firm. If, as these women often are, she is a bit of a martyr and observes when she sees you taking a sun bath, "I don't see how you can waste all that time when you know you have that stack of work on your desk," simply smile and say, "Of course not." There is always the chance, of course, that however under the weather she seems, emotionally, she's much happier working herself to death than she would be enjoying life. Some people can only be happy being miserable. It's a dreadful state to be in, but since they won't be helped, the best thing to do is to avoid being pulled in with them.

KEEP IT IN PROPORTION

For the one who allows herself to be pushed and pulled by whatever mood she finds herself in, laughter is the best medicine. In fact, a sense of humor is the greatest part of a sense of proportion. Appreciating the funny episodes in life, the really ridiculous things we do and say and get involved in, is seeing the distortion of proportion. The comic who has his audience helpless with laughter while he solemnly reduces a Model T Ford to a pile of junk in futile rage when it won't start makes us howl because his reaction is inconsistent with the cause of his anger.

Laurel and Hardy were masters at this sort of humor. Remember these sequences? Laurel accidentally tripped Hardy, who reacted by pushing Laurel into a puddle, who in turn reacted by pouring a bucket of water on Hardy's head, who . . . and so the ridiculous grew to the grotesque, and because it was so preposterous, everyone laughed. In a way, we were laughing at that part of ourselves that overreacts to situations, as we saw it expressed in ludicrous extremes.

We all demonstrate our innate sense of the fitness of things when, in the midst of a quarrel or discussion, or in listening to someone relate an experience, we say, "Oh, come now—don't be ridiculous!" What we are saying, in essence, is, "Keep it in proportion, can't you? This is out of balance."

There are times when it seems cruel to chuckle at the overwrought emotions of a friend who is really suffering, even though it is evident that the cause is not worth the trauma. We may be tempted to nod sympathetically, and, in fact, that's what most of us do when we are caught in such a situation. It's so easy to simply slide away from the subject by muttering, "Um—hum," rather than risk more emotions, the raised voice and strident tones of someone frustrated in the search for an ally.

We evade being honest in such situations because we dislike offending people, and the truth is often offensive. All our social training leads us to be gracious at the expense of absolute truth. But aren't there differences in social encounters that ought to temper our desire to be tactful? I admit it would be unkind and even uncalled for to go around telling our friends how much we dislike their clothes or make-up or personal traits; but that's not the same as agreeing with a friend who is deeply depressed over some small incident better forgotten. In the first instance, an opinion is produced without being asked for and usually is in regard to an unimportant detail. Who cares whether you like or dislike my choice of lipstick? But when my good friend comes in and tells me she has been on the verge of tears all day because the boss was unusually curt and she is afraid he isn't satisfied with her work, I believe it would be cowardly and wrong not to attempt to get her into a more positive frame of mind.

"It may have nothing to do with you at all," a woman once said to a girl with just that problem. "He may have had a fight with his wife that morning or be catching a cold or be worried about business. Are you doing the best job you can?"

"Oh, yes," she sniffed. "I know I make mistakes from time to time, but I'm conscientious and I don't goof the same way twice. It's just that he was *so* grumpy this morning, he . . ."

"Stop!" her friend yelled. "For heaven's sake are you going to go through your whole life letting other people's moods dictate yours? If you want to be blue, be blue—but do it on your own account for a real reason and not just because your boss is less than sunny once in a while. Let the poor man have his moods without making them worse by dripping around the office like a soap opera heroine. He may need to be lifted out of his mood, and you'd drown him in it."

She laughed a little at that and they went out to lunch. Her boss's bad temper eventually passed; she

23

never found out the cause, but it couldn't have been due to any dissatisfaction with her since she got a nice raise not long after. It's better, I believe, to say to someone brooding over a minor problem, "It's probably not nearly as serious as you think," than to imply by your sympathy—or silence—that the problem may indeed be grave and to be blue about it quite logical.

ADMIT THE BLUES EXIST

The third group of people who don't cope with minor depressions are those Christians whose philosophy doesn't permit them to admit they exist. There has always been a temptation to equate the victory Christ won for us over sin and death with the elimination of any kind of trouble at all. This is not biblical and certainly flies in the face of all Christ taught, as well as all human experience.

Victory is ultimately ours, it is true—but victory implies a battle, and that is exactly what this life is. We are not "let off" from the temptations and distresses of life, but we are assured that we will never be defeated by them. And the eventual victory doesn't mean that we won't lose some skirmishes from time to time. We get hurt, as other people do. We get sick and have disappointments in love and are betrayed by friends and cheated by those we have trusted. At such times it's inevitable that we be depressed and upset. There's a *reason* to be blue.

The Christian who believes in constant victory over all of life's distresses, however, can't cope with his depression because he can't admit that it's there. The

24

small, rather circumscribed view he has of God's purpose in the world won't permit him to face reality, and so there is no way for him to handle any of his emotional problems. Such a person is afraid, you see, that the presence of any emotion less than utter serenity would be, somehow, an admission of defeat as far as his faith is concerned. Nothing could be further from the truth. Faith isn't a soothing syrup poured into us and smothering all human emotions so that we feel nothing and are wafted through life in a kind of euphoria. It's a conviction that God can be trusted regardless of the circumstances, that He will never let what happens to us destroy our relationship with Him and our eventual victory.

One woman said to me years ago, in talking about this very subject, "I am never blue—never. Christ has given me absolute serenity at all times." I questioned her, but she stuck to her point as if she were being asked to recant the faith. I never did believe her, however, and could not help noticing that whenever she was under stress for any length of time she put on a lot of weight. She may not have been blue, but she evidently needed food as a comfort in times of tension. I believe it is better to admit you aren't always on top and look for the reasons for the depression rather than pretend it's not even there.

THE BIG AND THE LITTLE

A major cause of the blues—merely a light shade of blue, it's true, but still making one less than balanced —is the result of tasks too big, demands too heavy so that it seems impossible to ever get the mess straightened out. It's the way a woman feels when she gets up in the morning and sees so much work to be done around the house that a day's work will barely make a dent.

There's only one way to attack the problem and that is by reducing it to small jobs. Dr. Lindquist, when he was pastor of the First Presbyterian Church of Hollywood, used to advise his people to make a practice of breaking their various jobs into manageable units. Whatever it is, the job gets done bit by bit, and you have to start somewhere.

Whether it is a major undertaking, involving the work of other people and a complex organization, or one of the everyday tasks which have to be done repeatedly, the first thing is to decide how to break it up so as to get it done. I wish I could tell you about some impressive project which I handled this way, but most of my experiences have to do with more mundane things. However, these are worth respect as well as intelligent planning. Housework not handled in an organized manner can end up burying the housewife, not to mention her hapless husband and children, in a mountain of dirty dishes, unwashed clothes and hopelessly jumbled closets. These seemingly trivial jobs can become impossible burdens at which one stares in hopeless depression—unless they are disposed of with some efficiency.

It can all sound so banal, I know, especially in these days when any woman worth her salt is supposed to be out demanding her rights and being heard on important issues instead of merely keeping her home from chaos. Notice that the key word in that sentence was "merely"? It implies that keeping home from chaos is intrinsically worthless—a mere nothing. Used that way the word becomes an attack—a very subtle one— on whatever the speaker wishes to discount. Just precede it by the word "merely."

When you come right down to it, running a home so that the family is comfortable in more than physical aspects; so that food is well cooked, meals are pleasant, belongings are accessible, and the atmosphere is warm and welcoming—that's a major contribution to the health of society. Why are we so timid about being housewives? We even shun the word, opting for more "tony" descriptions like "homemaker." I don't like the word "homemaker." It smacks of cozy little articles in women's magazines designed to buck me up, and that's somehow rather patronizing.

Running a house is like running a business or a factory or a school or any other organization, with one major difference: The people who come home to that house every night will be more deeply affected by what goes on there than by any other group they will ever belong to. What we do in our homes is very, very important. We all like to think of ourselves as having some worthwhile impact on the world in which we live, and may miss our chance if we fail to realize that the influence we have on husbands and children and friends gives us more scope for being helpful— or damaging—than anything else we might do.

Now, admittedly, the way the house is run—the organization of it—isn't the main purpose of a home. Some women think it is, the way some office managers think the business exists to serve the typists and bookkeeping system. No, the organization of housework in all its aspects is necessary so the really important things that go on in a home can take place without being constantly impeded by confusion. Organization is like a skeleton—bare and ugly all by itself, but it holds the body together.

Many of the women I know who are depressed, some of them seriously, about the housework they never can manage have an aggrieved attitude about the situation. They feel it isn't fair that they should be so confined by the demands of running a home, that the countless jobs which need doing every day are interrupting the real work—the real contribution they see themselves making as wives and mothers. They are right. These repetitious little duties do take time and keep us from other things, but we are not the only ones who have to put up with such jobs. In a business, the constant telephone interruptions and the questions regarding procedures and the quarrels between employees which have to be handled take time from the main thrust of the business, whatever it is. But someone has to handle these matters.

Every administrator in a school knows that he spends a disproportionate amount of time in handling picayune details that have absolutely nothing to do with the main thrust of the school—educating people.

The Lighter Shades of Blue

But no education at all will take place if someone doesn't solve all the little problems before they become big problems. If you become frustrated and depressed over broken dishwashers and daily dusting and drawers that look as if they were stirred with a stick, you're not alone. As a secretary you'd be faced with the necessity of coping with different problems, and even the most glamorous professions are beset by minor irritations. Artists have to spend time stretching their canvas, and getting out—or putting away—their oils and supplies and cleaning brushes, which to them must be as mundane as doing the dishes every day.

Part of the depression some women feel as they contemplate their own situation is the feeling that getting it done really doesn't matter. It will only have to be done again. But it does matter, because having things well ordered and serene and clean makes a good atmosphere, which is what home is all about. And, in contrast, letting things slide doesn't mean you do the same thing tomorrow you might have done today—it means you work twice as hard and twice as long, because mess is accumulative. If a little mess today means a mild case of the blues, twice as much tomorrow may mean a crying jag and a trip to the drugstore to get something for the headache.

GETTING ORGANIZED

Well, back to the means of reducing these necessary tasks to manageable units. First, decide what has to

29

be done every day. Then decide what comes first, second, and so on. Allot time according to priorities. For instance, if you have a six-room house to straighten up, vacuum and dust every day, it would be foolish to spend hours every morning polishing silver and relining drawers and brooding over the recipe books. Get the necessary and daily jobs done first. Then, if there's time left over, you can take on the special projects which are so much fun. If you don't have time to do everything you'd like to do, decide what is most important to your whole family and get those things done first. Some people can put up with a dusty house if things are just put away; others are driven mad by a speck of dust, and don't mind magazines and papers lying about. Whichever way you—and your family—are geared, go that way.

My experience has been that in doing the things I have to do around the house a method evolves which eventually makes me more efficient in my use of time and frees me for other things. The great thing is to get at it and tackle it one thing at a time. Since this is not a book on how to clean and run a house, there isn't too much more I can tell you. If you are one of these women who really don't have the foggiest notion of how to organize your housework, then talk to someone who does.

On the other hand, if you have never had any trouble knowing how to run your home and are feeling impatient at the amount of space I've devoted to it, hold your fire. Several months ago I was invited to speak on this very subject at a large suburban church, and the crowd of women was enormous—and most of them were young. Some of the questions they asked indicated that many really did not know the first thing about keeping house, and a surprisingly large number said that their ineptness often made them profoundly depressed.

But when one is blue because of something as easily taken care of as a lack of organization there is hope. Please don't say pathetically, "But you don't understand—I'm just not an organized person." That's a spineless, cowardly approach to life. Being well-organized isn't a matter of talent, like singing or dancing; it's a matter of ability and some have more than others. But like the ability to get out of bed, take a daily bath, and be polite to people, it can be acquired. Most of our lives are spent doing things that don't come naturally; we've been taught. Just as we do not all have the same degree of skill in reading or mathematics, we will not all reach the same level of organizational ability. But everyone can develop some skill, and most of us can become better than we are now.

One final word about how we handle the less-serious causes of the blues. Regardless of the origin, when a depression persists over a long period of time, or when it is accompanied by physical fatigue, see the doctor *first*. No matter what the trouble is, it can't be handled if one is physically unable to muster up the energy.

This seems obvious, but isn't always. One friend of mine went through a period of several years during which she was constantly depressed. She couldn't seem to rise above her moods, and this inability to cope with herself made her still more low spirited. She prayed, she went to professional counselors, she tried desperately; but there was no improvement until a physician discovered she was in dire need of a hysterectomy. When told about her low state of mind he exclaimed, "Of course! Her condition produces depression. It's a wonder she's been able to function at all." There was a happy outcome—the surgery she underwent was the solution not only of her physical problem but of her depression as well.

We all have enough reasons, from time to time, to be blue; if we're in good physical health, we can usually handle our fluctuating moods. But it takes energy to do it. A physical checkup ought to be the first action one takes in coping with persistent depression.

CHAPTER THREE

Patches of Blue

There are times when it would be abnormal not to be a little bit blue—when there's a reason to feel depressed. Most of us, in the midst of such an experience, just get through it as best we can. Better than nothing, but not much better. Although there are times when one can do nothing to change the situation, quite often some action can be taken.

DEFEATING HOUSEWORK

For every woman who is blue because she doesn't know how to organize her housework there must be five who can do it very well but hate every minute of it. No matter how efficiently they run their homes, they are depressed because it's all so distasteful to them. This is frustrating, for unlike an office or factory job, you can't quit and get another one you like better. The only real solution seems to be a maid, and that's a financial impossibility for most of us, even if maids were to be found.

It's dangerous to do nothing about the blues one gets over housework because one can so easily slide into resentment toward the very people one cleans the house for. When my children were small my determination to have the house clean at all times tumbled me into that very thing. I found myself screaming at the children for tracking dirt into the house, for splashing water out of the bathtub, for putting their hands on the walls—in short, for just about every move they made. I hated myself for being such a fishwife but couldn't stop it.

No dramatic incident causing me to suddenly see the light took place. I didn't overhear my children in one of those touching conversations that make such wonderful stories, though I imagine if I *had* heard some of their comments about me, I'd have been horrified. No, it simply occurred to me one day when I was indulging in a bit of foul temper—I think I kicked the vacuum—that I was letting myself be defeated by jobs so small and so ordinary that they took very little brain power. Here I was, a fairly intelligent woman, allowing objects—mere things—to determine my moods, to alter the very shape of my days. It suddenly seemed quite ridiculous. I decided I would no longer be controlled by my work, I would control it.

That sounds very trivial, but it was a momentous decision. There was no overnight change, of course. I did not wake up the next morning and bound out of bed or sing cheery little songs while I dusted. Housework is not very interesting and never will be. But the determination not to let it set my temperament for the day did bring about an eventual and permanent change in my attitude.

It is possible to decide what one will think about while cleaning, since the things one does around the house require very little thought. I had been thinking about how I hated what I was doing; now I thought about other things, and you'd be surprised how much I accomplished while getting through the daily jobs.

There were immediate rewards for my new point of view. I was less tired, for one thing, which surprised me until I realized what a tremendous amount of energy I had been spending on the blues. Being depressed is very enervating. Then I began to enjoy the children more and I am sure they enjoyed me more. Finally, my husband was happier and said so. I must have been dreadful to come home to, and I can only be thankful that he was a man of integrity, committed to me and the children, or he would surely have found someone more fun to be with long before. You see, for every dissatisfied housewife who wishes she were doing something more glamorous there are two single women who would give their eyeteeth to be married and keeping house—and those women are out there in the business world meeting the husbands who go home to petulant, resentful wives. No wonder men stray so often. The moral is plain to be seen— whatever you have to do around the house to keep your husband happy, do it. Running a house competently is no more exceptional than any other job and, I suspect, no more depressing.

THE FRAZZLE OF FINANCES

The patches of blue that color our lives from time to time have one thing in common—there is a definable cause. That's what is so hopeful about them. There is the possibility of a solution when the problem is known. A change of attitude, perhaps, as when I made up my mind not to let my emotional health be decided by something so trivial as housework. More often the depression can be routed by action—something must be done to help the situation.

Or take money, for instance—I suppose that the one worry plaguing more of us than any other is the perennial fret about money. Few of us have enough of it, many of us know we don't handle money very well and the whole subject makes us tremble with inadequacy. Beginning with my first efforts to learn to count, when my father lost his temper each time I bogged down at "three," I have had a serious mental block about mathematics, which led to my being inept with money. The very thought of balancing my checkbook and reconciling the bank statement used to make me break out into a light perspiration. How I worried about it!

There will never come a time, I suspect, when my heart doesn't sink just a trifle as I pull the bank statement envelope out of the mailbox, but at least at this point I have the situation under control. It just wasn't worth getting the blues over, and I have some suggestions that may be helpful. They may strike the financial experts as heresy, but I do not expect financial experts to be reading this book anyway. They are immersed in *The Wall Street Journal* and the daily stock market reports.

First of all, everything in our society conspires to put—and keep us—in utter, abject subjection to money. The possession of money and all it can buy as a standard of success has been so well discussed and deplored there is no need to say more about it. However, discussion about the evils of materialism has not, so far, changed our values very much. The world— that is the world outside the Christian faith—will always be enamored of money because it represents power and prestige as well as the ease of living we tend to feel is ours by right.

Christians who believe that who we are is more important than how much we own will always be a very small minority, and we will always be surrounded on all sides by a culture that worships money. Our job is to keep ourselves as free of that standard as we can, which means constant vigilance. The reward of that vigilance is great, however; it means we can be free of the persistent depression that clouds our lives when we allow money to be our standard of success. When a man feels he's a failure because he isn't making so much money that his family just can't spend it all, he's always under a cloud. Therefore, the first and necessary step is to decide that money is not the standard of success. Being a real person, as genuine before God as we humans can ever be, is far more important.

Secondly—and this is against absolutely every financial precept of our times—I don't make a habit of buying things on credit. The almost overwhelming sense of freedom, of relaxation, that I experienced when I quit buying on time was worth anything I did without.

There are a few major exceptions, of course. We are buying a house and have a mortgage. I'd like to pay it off, though every financial advisor we've talked to screams at the very idea. I don't know enough about finance to argue with them when they tell me my money can make more for me invested in something than in paying off a house, but I sometimes wonder if those men ever think of anything—houses, wives, children, friends—except in terms of investment.

But as for lesser purchases, the only way for me to avoid being always a little strung out over money worries is to pay cash for what I buy. That means I wait until I can actually afford something—imagine that!—before I buy it. What comes next is possibly even more radical to the American buying public. I don't see why it's necessary to be forever making huge payments in order to have a new car every other year. An automobile well taken care of ought to last more than two years, and mine has. It's a 1959 Mercedes 220 convertible and was not new when I bought it. It is the most beautiful body ever built, to my way of thinking, and that's why I got it, besides the fact that it's a nice tidy car—it doesn't stretch from curb to curb and goes around corners neatly. I expect to be driving it when I'm a crotchety old lady of ninety, if I live that long. If it seems like heresy to own a foreign car instead of an American product, all I can say is that at thirteen years of age it is still solid, the doors close tightly, everything works, and when someone can show me a better bargain I'll buy it. The great gift I get from owning an old car is that I am under no pressure to keep my nose to the grindstone in order to pay for an expensive status symbol.

My final gesture of defiance at the specter of the money blues takes the form of deciding—deliberately —not to spend any time fretting about financial situations I can't change. My husband and I will never be wealthy; college professors and writers seldom are. On the other hand, we both enjoy what we are doing and that's worth more than all the gold in Fort Knox, if there is still any there.

You see, the joker in the money-as-the-measure-of-happiness cult is that there is nothing that can vanish more quickly. Conditions suddenly change, the economic picture alters and what looked to be a solid investment turns to nothing but paper. Money is necessary to maintain life, and the best way to get it is to work for it doing something you enjoy doing, but it isn't worth moping over.

NOBODY'S PERFECT

Next to money the most common cause of a temporary fit of the blues is a misunderstanding between friends or lovers. When a relationship sours, it's impossible not to be depressed. Something good, something necessary to happiness, has gone awry. Still, the situation is not hopeless. What has gone wrong can often be put right, and at this point we may discover that something other than friendship lies at the root of the trouble. Bad feelings seldom arise out of temperamental difficulties; they are caused by some point at which each person demands his rights and refuses to give way.

One woman used to follow a recognizable pattern with each friendship. She was first enamored of a new friend and spent as much time with her as she could. Then, as they began to know one another better, she was disappointed in the flaws she found and inclined to withdraw from the friendship. There would follow a period of coolness. Often the friend would retaliate by being very chilly herself, and oddly enough, this always hurt the woman deeply. Eventually the relationship deteriorated completely, and she began the same process with someone else. Her failure to sustain a good relationship grew out of her inability to accept friendship on a level less than ideal. The friend had to be available on her terms, had to remain perfect on her terms. In short, she could not accept reality—the thorny combination of good and bad we live with.

There's no help for her or for those who demand perfection of a relationship short of settling for reality. Once one learns to accept people as they are without demanding perfection of them, relationships can deepen and grow. If that isn't done, then the on-again-off-again process will go with its accompanying times of the blues.

40

Patches of Blue

Friendship, like love, is absolutely necessary to happiness for most of us, and yet it, like love, is the source of much of our unhappiness. We either haven't friends and are miserable because of the lack or a friend disappoints and betrays or a misunderstanding breaks what had been a satisfying relationship. All this is quite natural considering the complex persons we all are, with motives and drives and needs often at odds with each other. In any case, when something goes wrong with a friendship, depression is the result.

I believe it's better to do something about the cause of the depression rather than wallow in it, and that is where some will part company with me. There are those, unfortunately, who would rather be miserable than become vulnerable enough to try to set things straight. "I have my pride," they say, "and if she doesn't want my friendship, I certainly won't force it upon her. Let her come to me—she's the one who . . ." and the list of grievances goes on.

The title of this chapter is "Patches of Blue," and when it comes to friendship there will inevitably be such patches. We are faulty human beings and we will, from time to time, find ourselves at odds with those who matter a great deal to us—either because of our own failings or because others, like us, are not perfect. The result will be a period of unhappiness—temporary, like most of our depressions, because the misunderstanding or disagreement will eventually be resolved.

41

IT'S UP TO YOU

There is one frightening exception to this rule, and that occurs when one of the parties to the disagreement is unable to admit culpability. It seems incredible that anyone at all could be so locked in conceit and self-esteem as not to be able to make amends for having been in the wrong; but the world is full of unhappy human beings in that very predicament. They are miserable and always slightly depressed because they never have been able to sustain a good relationship on any level. But for all their misery they will go on being depressed, winding themselves ever tighter in their little cocoon of resentment and self-justification because the misery of being alone and neglected is, to them, better than the misery of humbling themselves to admit a wrong.

It is not overstating the case to say all this. All of us have known such people. They appeal to us for partisanship, they tell interminably long tales of wrongs inflicted on them by others, and they are desperately unhappy. But they demand that all relationships exist on their terms, that everyone—friends, relatives, lovers—accept all responsibility for the relationship and that they themselves must always be absolved from any guilt when things go wrong.

These people are sometimes Christians—at least they say they are—but one wonders how anyone so totally unable to admit blame in a human relationship could accept the fact that he is guilty before God. The first requirement for becoming a Christian is that one accept the fact that no one, on his own merits, has any right to stand before God. We are, as the Bible tells us, all sinners. If we are all sinners and becoming a Christian is predicated on accepting that fact and then accepting Christ's intervention on our behalf, how ridiculous to refuse to admit sin in any particular instance.

Yet it happens. Again and again one finds friendships broken because of the pride and haughtiness (old-fashioned but accurate descriptions) of one person. These people would rather be depressed on their terms than happy on God's terms. They may belong to Him—only He can say—but they do not behave like His people, and they show no evidences of His work in their lives.

There is no ease for the unhappiness, the continuing depression these people suffer. They suffer by their own choice, and there is no cure other than admitting they are often at fault, just as culpable as others and so needing forgiveness—and that they will not do. It is too bad to conclude a chapter on such a somber note, but the fact remains that for those who demand that all relationships be on their terms with any blame for differences being assumed by others, life will be a succession of broken relationships and consequent unhappiness.

CHAPTER FOUR

How Did I Get This Way?

This is a dangerous point in our book because the moment one begins to bring the question, "Where did it all begin," from the general (the Garden of Eden and the fall) to the particular (but why am *I* the way I am?), one is faced with the current unassorted and heterogeneous mixture of psychological notions. There is an immediate mental picture of the psychiatrist's couch and probing into the past along with the implication that all the hang-ups in the world can be explained on the basis of some childhood trauma.

I don't believe that. There is truth, of course, in the theory that early experiences in life have exerted profound influences on all of us. We are, most of us, the product of all our impressions, experiences, environmental influences and so on—within limits. We are also human beings created by God and every one of us is unique. Part of our uniqueness is the result of heredity and environment. but it is, nonetheless, unique. We are thinking, feeling, deciding human beings and we make choices.

FREEDOM OF CHOICE

The determinist tells us that even our choices are not free, they are the result of factors beyond our control, so that one's destiny is decided not by the individual but by all that went into making him what he is. The Bible views man as *more* than a collection of genes and chromosomes and environmental influences. He is a being capable of choice. Even though we are born into a sinful world, none of us starting life in a perfect situation, we are not robots, forced to follow the dictates of whatever nature heredity has provided us any more than Adam and Eve were robots, forced to choose the good. They chose wrongly, even in a perfect situation. We do not have the clear-cut choice between good and evil they had; our choices are usually between shades of gray rather than black and white. But we have enough comprehension of goodness in us to distinguish between these shades and to choose what is closer to absolute right. That, in short, is the doctrine of general revelation.

Paul writes in his letter to the Romans that men are responsible for their actions. "It is not that they do not know the truth about God; indeed he has made it quite plain to them. For since the beginning of the world the invisible attributes of God, e.g., his eternal power and divinity, have been plainly discernible through things which he has made and which are commonly seen and known, thus leaving these men without a rag of excuse."

The Bible sees man as infected by sin and yet able

46

to glimpse, however imperfectly, the good that God demands. He cannot live up to it though he may try. But he has the ability to decide and is required to decide for good rather than evil. His decision will never be perfectly right. But in a world where some men and some causes are far more right than others, we must choose that which is closest to the perfection we see but cannot ever quite reach.

Furthermore, the Bible teaches that the Holy Spirit is active in the world, that whenever there is the slightest yearning on the part of a man or woman to know God the Spirit of God seizes that opportunity and gives power to accept what God has done for us in Christ.

The determinists are right in saying that all of us are the product of centuries of history, heredity, conditioning and culture, but wrong in saying they are the only factors having any influence on us. God is and He is active. This teaching of the Bible is corroborated in the experience of all who have come to know Christ. We are conscious of all the facets of our own temperaments that predispose us toward certain attitudes, as well as of yearnings and needs that are contrary. There comes a time when these inborn tendencies may conflict with our longings, and at such times we choose—and we know beyond a shadow of a doubt that we are choosing with a *third* something. Neither our natural tendencies nor our hopes or fears are doing the choosing. It's something else, and that something else is what we call "I." The real person,

47

the person who may have inherited traits and environmental conditioning but who is more than the sum of both of them. That real person chooses.

THE PROBLEM OF TEMPERAMENT

Having said all that, it is true that one's inherited temperament and intelligence and physical equipment have a bearing on life. After all, that is the equipment we have to work with. But it is only equipment, and it is modified and even altered by many things, not the least among them our own ability to choose.

My own temperament is introspective, fearful, proud. As a small child I was afraid of a great many things, from whatever lurked in the dark at night to the thundering anger of my father. I hated being wrong; perhaps at home being wrong meant a severe spanking accompanied by steely anger on the part of my father and on my part a desolate feeling of being outside his love.

The whole business of living was becoming highly complicated. Before I went to school I realized that to be loved meant meeting performance standards. My parents had one standard, and it was hard enough to live up to it. The children in the neighborhood often had another and to be rejected by them was painful indeed. How dreadful were the times when their standards demanded that I behave in a way that contradicted my parents' standards! Then the choice—and even at that time I was learning the agonies of choosing —was between suffering the wrath and punishment of my parents or that of my friends.

How Did I Get This Way?

Sometime during those very early years I became aware of God, who also cared about my choices. In a very dim, hardly formulated way, I began to suspect that neither my parents' demands nor those of my friends were always synonymous with what God wanted.

Later on, in school, it became even more complex. Teachers had their own standards of performance, and now in order to have my tiny universe in order, it was necessary to please (1) God, (2) my parents, (3) my friends and (4) my teachers. I think this is a common perhaps universal experience. We are realizing our own identity little by little, in relationship with others while at the same time discovering the bewildering world of human relationship and its demands on us.

You can see that few of us will be without some anxieties about our acceptability; by the time we are adults we have found, often painfully, that performance according to the demands of the individuals in our lives is the way to be accepted. How very natural, in view of this, that we should often be depressed. Depression, after all, is never the sole emotion, at least not until it has gotten beyond the pale of the normal and has become pathological. It is always induced by other emotions which we may or may not be aware of. In actuality, it may effectively mask the real trouble so that while we are worrying about being blue we are avoiding the real menace behind our blues—fear.

The performance standards themselves have a great deal to do with the form any particular anxiety will take. The girl whose mother wants nothing more for her than that she be pretty, popular and marry well may be consumed with fear of failing in these areas, while another girl whose parents demand excellence in school, and who just cannot come up to their expectations, will be anxious about failure as a student.

IT'S YOUR DECISION

There is no doubt that some of us are just naturally inclined more toward a somewhat depressed view of life than others. In spite of the assumption that modern psychiatry can, if applied, eliminate all problems and solve all difficulties so that we are all equally well balanced, that just isn't possible. What it can do is to help us to cope with the temperaments we all are born with, as well as whatever modifications our backgrounds have made.

Since I'm not writing from the point of view of the psychologist or psychiatrist, I'd like to reduce the problem of temperament to its simplest form. Granted, we all have inherited tendencies as well as learned behavior patterns. But neither of these factors is the controlling factor.

We all have feelings, the ability to love, some idea of right and wrong. The one ingredient in human beings that makes us free and not mere robots is that we have the power to choose. I have heard people talk about their problems and their sessions with their psychiatrists, and it all comes out sounding as if whatever their situations, they were totally passive in them. I just can't accept that.

From the time one is very small the necessity for choosing, for making decisions, is present. Parents may be able to force some sort of compliance with their rules, a compliance that is resented and will be thrown off as soon as possible. But no one can force anyone else to have a certain attitude. In the realm of our own inner lives—the stance we take when we are alone and not conforming to social regulation—we are free to choose.

It was a long time before I realized what an important part of my life that ability to choose for myself was. No matter what happened to me, whether my husband was considerate or gruff, *I* could decide what my own attitude would be.

"But," one friend said to me, "that's just not true. I can't *help* being depressed. I don't choose to; I'm miserable. But I can't stop it; I'm helpless." She was absolutely right as far as her feelings went, but she still had the power to decide whether or not to give in to them. She could sit immobile on her sofa and sink deeper into her mood, or she could get up, walk to the front door and go out of the house—shopping or gardening or to have coffee with a neighbor.

There comes a time when one cannot choose, of course—when weeks and months and perhaps years of giving in to whatever the mood is have formed a behavior pattern too strong to break. But before that

51

happens there are opportunities, day after day, to break a bad-behavior pattern, to make a decision that will change the whole setting in which a mood develops. That's what's important for us to know—that long before anyone gets to the point where only a psychiatrist or psychologist can help us, *we* have the power to help ourselves. And that means making decisions.

One man told me that all his life he had reacted to any kind of conflict in just one way—he walked out. He turned his back on friendships, on romances, on jobs, whenever an argument or disagreement developed. His life was littered with broken relationships. He hated what he was doing but was powerless to change the ingrained, ever-deepening habit of just running away from difficulties in relationships. That did not change until he made a conscious decision to run his life differently.

The decision to do that came because he had become a Christian, but that does not mean it was either automatic or easy. It's a very difficult, painful matter to alter the way one has reacted, to subdue instinctive reactions and habits of thinking; but he did it. He had to decide that he would rather cope with the pain and difficulty of wrenching himself out of old behavior patterns than with the continued misery of fractured relationships.

"REAP A CHARACTER"

We may laugh at aphorisms and trite sayings, but they are all true. They have become "old saws" because of their truth, so evident that they were repeated until they were clichés. One of them fits this topic perfectly: "Sow a thought, reap an action; sow an action, reap a habit; sow a habit, reap a character." That's the way it works, and the rule holds true in matters of temperament just as it does in any other area of life. Whatever one's emotional equipment for life is—bouncy and energetic, lethargic, mercurial in changing from laughter to temper—it can be modified, and it is done by making minute decisions many times a day.

Parents, when they reward their children for behaving well and punish them when they are naughty, are trying to encourage the child to make the right choices in life. Really smart parents offer their children alternatives instead of punishment, just as soon as the child is old enough. By that I mean that when a child is very small there's no use in reasoning with him; he can't understand. When a toddler throws a tantrum and beats his head on the floor he's not amenable to reason. I believe the best way to handle such an action is to leave him alone, really alone. That deprives him of the reward of the tantrum, which is attention even if it does mean mother gets upset and screams and spanks him, then cries. The punishment is suited to the crime, so to speak, and is the forerunner of later training, which will show the child that it's better to choose to regulate his temper than to give in to it.

We've all known adults who have never learned to control some basic emotional behavior pattern and who suffer—as do their families and friends—because of it. At fifty it's a little late to learn how to get busy with a project that will help one out of the blues, or to control one's temper or not to go into the sulks at every disappointment—but at five, or ten, or the teens or even into the twenties and thirties it can be done. The important thing is to make the right choices now —before it is too late.

It appears that in attempting to answer the question, "How did I get this way?" we have leaped from a quick and necessarily superficial analysis of our make-up to the conclusion that we have the ability to make decisions that will bring about change. This is no doubt frustrating to one who wants either a detailed examination of all that goes into the making of a person with problems or ten neatly listed rules of things to do.

Analyzing and probing into one's background and heredity can be very comforting. It enhances the conviction which tempts us all—that whatever our temperament is, it's not our fault. And when one is really serious about climbing out of the slough of the blues it's awfully nice to have some rules. We feel that if we just follow them closely enough all will be well; like taking the medicine as directed.

To be told, therefore, that we all have the ability to make decisions that will alter the course of our lives is like a dash of cold water in the face when you expected a pat on the back.

"But *what* choices?" is the natural reaction. The plain fact is that no one can tell anyone else what

54

to do. All that will help is to be given all the facts possible about all the alternatives offered—and then it's up to each one of us. I am convinced that there is enough general knowledge of what is good and right and helpful around so that no one has to make his choices in a vacuum. They won't be perfect— God doesn't demand that; only that we do the best we can with what we have.

CHAPTER FIVE

The Hidden Adversary

The first reaction most of us have when we meet a despondent friend is to try to cheer him up. Since emotions are so contagious, we instinctively feel that either we must succeed in helping him lift the mood or we ourselves will be brought down to it. Certainly there is nothing harder to bear than the company of one who will *not* be cheered up, who responds to every effort in that direction by a dreary repetition of his troubles. Inevitably, he will be left pretty much alone, and that deepens his melancholy still further.

ACCEPT YOURSELF

Of the people I have known who were habitually low spirited there have been more whose depression stemmed from self-hatred than all other causes. Some of them were quite open about it—they loathed themselves and they knew why. The melancholy view of life resulting from their inability to accept themselves was a cry for help.

"Show me that things aren't so bad," were the unspoken words between the lines of all their complaints. "Show me that perhaps *I'm* not so bad and then I may be able to find something to be happy about." The one thing these unhappy people need is to be loved and wanted; and they make it very difficult for anyone to love them. It takes rigorous persistence to overlook the whining note of self-pity or the apologetic pushiness with which these wretches meet every attempt at friendship. And yet they need it so desperately.

One woman used to greet me with the same sentence every time I saw her: "Well, I'm sure you're tired of seeing me!" I did get very tired indeed of assuring her that I was not tired of seeing her, and angrily conscious of the fact that I felt constrained to be overly friendly lest she imagine herself to be unwanted. Although she would have denied it vehemently, I felt she was using her despondency to manipulate me. She knew very well what effect her self-abnegation had on others, and she played on our unwillingness to hurt her. Even so, nothing we did was enough to convince her she was really wanted.

Most of her friends eventually got tired of her insatiable need for reassurance and drifted away, which only made her worse. "You see—nobody likes me, I don't know why when I try so *hard,* but there's just something wrong with me I guess." And then the tears. When she got to this point I was always in a state of inner fury and frustration. She wanted me to sympathize with her, to tell her she was all right and whoever had given her the cold shoulder was

58

wrong, but that wasn't the truth. There *was* something wrong with her—such a low estimate of her own being as a person that she made no attempt to develop in any direction, offered nothing in a friendship except an almost indecent longing for acceptance.

In the end I told her just that. Not without apprehension, not without thoughtful prayers on the subject, but spurred on by the memory of my own past history when I had been prey to just such self-hatred. I knew very well how she felt, because I had felt that same way, said almost those same words. I remembered the friends who had pulled me out of that slough of despondency, and that they had done it with kindness and real love, but also with firmness. They told me, in short, that I was neither so lacking in attractiveness as I thought nor so unique in my self-doubt as I thought and to stop acting like a tragedy queen.

Paul wrote to the Ephesians that they were "meant to hold firmly to the truth in love, and to grow up in every way into Christ." One of the ways in which we grow up is to accept the fact that He loves us, and if He loves us, who are we to hold out? This may sound too simple. It's like all the most important issues of life, easy to say but much more difficult to do. I found it difficult but not impossible, and so did my friend. The difference to both of us was that we had someone who cared enough to tell the truth and say it out of enough love and concern to ease the sting. No one likes to be told that his self-hatred, which seems so humble—almost virtuous—is, in fact, a virulent kind of pride. But that is what self-hatred really is.

THE QUEST FOR PERFECTION

If one could put the underlying reason for self-hatred into one sentence it would be, "I can't bear it because I'm not absolutely perfect." To expect a great deal of oneself seems so virtuous, such an admirable trait, that we are inclined at first to admire these high-minded souls. It is only as we know them better that we see how cold and uncomfortable is the pride that prevents them from admitting any flaw or failure at all. It isn't a desire to be good or whole or kind or capable that drives them, it is a desire to be *better* than others.

I don't know how early the competitive spirit enters the thinking of most human beings, but I sometimes suspect that it's there from the beginning, one of the legacies of Adam's fall. "If I were only prettier than . . . or smarter than . . . or richer than . . ." is the way it goes. I know because I've felt that way and so, if you are honest, have most of you. The dreadful fruit of this particular obsession is the insidious desire to be "more than," which can never be satisfied. There's always someone prettier or smarter or richer. The quest is self-defeating.

It's also founded on totally false ideas of human love. We do not love people because they are pretty or smart or can sing well or are rich—or for any other virtue. We "just love them." It's always possible to enumerate all the reasons why one *doesn't* like or love someone, but not why one does. That's because affinity—rapport that exists in every good friendship and between good lovers—isn't reasonable. One can't analyze it, it is simply "just there."

To imagine, therefore, that if only one could be better than someone else one would have all kinds of friends and lovers is nonsense. Self-hatred is a sin as well as a sickness because it is a denial of one's own uniqueness. It says "No!" to God's creative power as well as His redeeming grace. In essence, it says, "I don't like the way you made me, and there is nothing you can do to help me."

I know that rejection of one's self can become so pathological that there is no help other than to go to a psychiatrist or psychologist, but I believe that that necessity is often the result of self-indulgence. I've known all too many women who would rather be unhappy and full of self-pity than do anything at all to change themselves. We are so accustomed to thinking of ourselves in terms of the psychologist that we often forget how many of our problems are the result of a childish refusal to help ourselves.

One college girl I knew told me quite seriously that she just couldn't seem to work hard in her classes because she wasn't "motivated." I asked her what she meant by that and she said vaguely, "Oh—you know —I just don't feel any—well, any *motivation.*" I suppose she meant that she expected to be propelled by an inner compulsion to get an education, or a fascina-

61

tion for history or literature. I think that's what many people are waiting for when it comes to doing anything about themselves. They won't act because they don't *feel* motivated; there is no overwhelming compulsion impelling them to action and so they do nothing. What nonsense!

In fact, with all the great good that the science of psychology has done for us, it also has a negative aspect which is the notion that we aren't responsible for what we are and do. We look for causes in our childhood or heredity, or attribute all our failings to traumatic experiences in life, as if we were not responsible or had no ability to think and choose. There's no doubt that we all are to some degree affected by our heredity and background and by the experiences of life, but we are more than computerized robots. The idea that we are nothing more than the sum total of what others have done to us is a pagan concept.

THE BAD AND THE GOOD

Out of it comes these two attitudes toward ourselves: first, that we aren't responsible for what we are because we are simply the product of all our early experiences; and secondly, that we needn't do anything at all unless there is some mysterious and indefinable urge we call "motivation." By that we usually mean an emotional—not intellectual—drive, or compulsion, which impels us to achieve. That also is something for which we're not responsible. It's just there—or it isn't, and if it isn't, then we can't be expected to do anything about it.

Perhaps this passive attitude toward life is as much the result of a changing moral climate as of a shallow, popular view of what psychology has to say about human beings. At any rate, psychology as an area of study certainly began to rise at the same time that traditional views of morality and ethics were being questioned. The result is, in the words of a current joke, "I've got some bad news and some good news."

The bad news is that anyone who is looking for an excuse for not becoming a responsible human being has it at hand in a popularized version of psychiatry, along with a skeptical attitude about many of the moral and ethical precepts. Situational ethics means, to such a person, that he really doesn't have to do anything he doesn't want to and as for the qualifying demand that he act in love, he's free to decide for himself what love is and that's usually what he already wants to do. And for the person who can't accept himself and is miserable about it, all he reads of psychology tells him that it's not his fault anyway and he can't be expected to change himself.

The good news is that psychology can help us understand ourselves if we use it as a tool and not as a religion. A skeptical attitude toward previously accepted standards of morals and ethics can lead—by virtue of stringent and honest examination—to a renewed allegiance to principles based on genuine morality. We have to accept the fact that a lot of what we used to call morality had nothing to do with biblical truth at all but was the outgrowth of a particular culture and might even be very bad.

We have to accept the bad along with the good and do what we can to minimize it. And one of the bad results of what we have been discussing is the reluctance of many people to look at themselves *where they are* and decide to do something about it. Every single one of the seriously depressed people I've known could not accept herself, and had a very poor self-image along with a strong feeling of self-pity. Every one, in spite of bemoaning her lack of abilities or character or virtues or personality, felt put upon because of her problems. She was not responsible, someone else was, and she certainly couldn't be expected to do anything about it.

SO WHY NOT CHANGE?

Quite often the self-hatred is accompanied by hostility which is so masked by depression that its presence is unsuspected. I knew one girl who was deeply unhappy. She really could find nothing good or lovable about herself, and she was sure no one else could either. And yet, along with her low opinion of herself went a determination to be accepted just the way she was. It sounds contradictory, and it is, but most of the people who are depressed because they can't accept themselves behave just as she did. She wanted friends desperately and clung to anyone who would listen to her at all—but it had to be on her terms, which were odd in the extreme.

The Hidden Adversary

The terms were that she must be always welcome, always listened to sympathetically, always comforted and jollied out of her depression, and when that failed—as it inevitably did—then her hostility became apparent.

She sank at such times into a sullen silence, a half-tearful grimace of despair which was apparent half a block away. She always said, "I know people don't like me; I know they get tired of me. Oh, I'm so depressed I'd just like to die." But there was as much cold rage as there was self-hatred. And she would not change.

"I *have* tried," she often said, "and I just can't change." There are two opinions one may have about her statement. It may have been true, and her emotional unease and low opinion of herself may have made her incapable of acting rightly. That is what most of us, affected as we are by the purely psychological view of humanity, would say. She was helpless and simply could not do what she knew to be right.

I don't believe it. I do not believe that anyone capable of thinking logically, holding a job and able to look at herself objectively is totally incapable of living up to the most minimal social standards of courtesy. She could have smiled and been pleasant when politeness demanded it, but she did not want to. She may not have been able to pull herself out of a depression, but she was able to behave with civility and chose, instead, to be unpleasant.

Her reasons for choosing not to exercise any sort of

self-control over her emotional state were no doubt somewhat chaotic. Everyone has enough negative experiences in his life by the time he is in his mid-twenties to give him some excuse for depression. The difference is not in the experiences of life but in how we allow them to affect us.

That is not to say there aren't great differences of temperament and heredity and experiences between people, differences that predispose some to more unstable emotion than others. But granted the differences, it's not always the people who have had every advantage and are blessed with open, uncomplicated lives and sunny dispositions who come through troubles with the least difficulty. It would be impossible to pinpoint whatever it is in the training or background of the ones who refuse to give in to depression, who may struggle with heartbreaking problems and yet maintain their serenity, or who come through an emotional storm with renewed strength. But since they have no similarities at all in heredity or background or advantages or lack of advantages, I would submit the assumption that they have one thing in common: They have learned to accept the responsibility of their own lives.

We go back to the point we discussed in Chapter Four: choices. The popular view of humanity is that all that has happened to us plus the hereditary emotional patterns we were born with somehow works together to determine the choices in life we'll make. My friend who was so depressed could not help being that way, nor could she do anything about it because she was the victim of all that had happened to her. The other view, which I believe to be true, is that our choices determine not only character and direction to life but also emotional health and, in some cases, mental health. It's possible to choose *not* to control one's emotions long enough so that a habit pattern is established and becomes very hard to break. In the end, one who lived like that could say truthfully, "I just can't help myself." But he could have helped himself time after time after time—and will be held responsible, according to the Bible, for all the times he chose wrongly.

A PERSONAL EXPERIENCE

It is with some hesitancy that I write of my own experience with depression, partly because I dislike the sort of overwrought confidences of personal experience often produced on this subject, and partly because it was painful enough and recalling it is not pleasant. However, that experience was the means by which I discovered that we really do have the power of choice, and that what we choose can make a difference in life.

All the ingredients to produce a classic case of depression were present in my life and could have been explained by any competent psychologist. Later, after that period of depression had been long gone, a psychologist did give me some insights into the roots of my trouble. It was interesting and helpful, in a rather detached way—much like hearing a lecture on child-hood diseases after one is grown. Discovering the reasons why I had become depressed, as I did at a time when life was fairly easy rather than during that difficult time, was the final *thunk* of earth on the grave of that experience. The burial was final.

The story may not be unlike yours or someone you know. My father, a good man—a very good man—who faced difficulties with a kind of grim determination not to be conquered, was inarticulate about his feelings. He could not show his wife or his children that he loved us. I grew up feeling that there must be something basically unlovable about me, and anyone who suspects he isn't lovable can look at himself and find reasons to support his belief. I wasn't especially pretty or bouncy and vivacious or good at sports or talented in any way.

My marriage at nineteen was to a man who, like my father, was very good, but also like my father not very articulate about how he felt. Any good psychiatrist could talk for several minutes on why I picked a man so like my father. The point is that as we began our marriage and the raising of our children the suspicion that I wasn't really the sort of woman who is loved very much persisted. I wasn't conscious of it, of course, and by the time I had become a Christian it was pushed down pretty firmly into my subconscious. After all, God loved me so why shouldn't I be able to accept the fact that others did too, whether they were verbal about it or not?

The Hidden Adversary

There were a few very hard years in our lives during the depression, World War II, and the years following. Illness, the small but consuming worries of raising a family, and in 1948 a polio epidemic that affected our two daughters. Donna, who was only four at the time, had a light case with minimal residual. Carole Ann, who was seven, was quite ill and needed therapy after the initial stay in the hospital of about six months. She did fairly well, although her stomach muscles were weak and necessitated her wearing a leather brace.

In late 1950 other alarming symptoms appeared. In February 1951 she was operated on for a brain tumor and died after two weeks during which time she never regained consciousness. Faith in the ultimate goodness of God became very real to me and to my husband then, in spite of circumstances that seemed to make nonsense of any belief in a loving, caring, concerned God.

In the fall of 1951 my husband was transferred to a midwestern city and that move was the straw that broke the camel's back. I began to sink into an alarming depression with all sorts of frightening symptoms, and after a few months we returned to California. I suppose my thought was that I'd be well again back home among old and dear friends and in surroundings where I'd been happy before. However, the move did not make me well and the depression continued.

It was about two years before I was free of it, and that without the aid of any professional psychologist,

69

not out of choice, but because at that time only very affluent people went to psychologists or psychiatrists and we were struggling to re-establish ourselves financially after the move back home. My friend Dr. Richard C. Halverson, who was on the staff of the Hollywood Presbyterian Church at the time, helped me greatly, far more than he knew since his theological studies had not included any psychology. His wife, Doris, a close friend, and Opal Hughes, another very dear friend, kept me going because of their friendship and understanding.

In the end (how simple it sounds, how complex it was) I began to recover. I never had a complete breakdown. I functioned normally as a wife and mother and I doubt if very many people had any idea at all of the torment seething inside me. Now that it is over, I can thank God for much of that time; it was painful, but I came out of it more sure of my faith than ever before.

Briefly, I never gave in or decided to give up. Whether it was inherited stubbornness or the spiritual virtue of endurance I do not know. Probably a little bit of both. The basis for my depression was, of course, a composite of many things. But probably the single strongest strand was the fear, buried very deeply for many years, that I was an unlovable person (my father, stern and apparently often angry with me, and my husband, demanding, not very verbal about his feelings for me) and if I were that unlovable then God would pay no attention to my prayers. The years of financial stress, the illnesses, Carole Ann's death—these must be all I deserved because there was something about me that demanded punishment.

AND VICTORY

All this was going on at the same time other kinds of awareness were taking place. I was learning something about Christian faith. I was gaining some insights into what it meant to be a Christian, however contradictory my fears of being unlovely were. It's not true that we are one-level persons, learning, growing in a straight line—one thing at a time. Instead, we are assimilating multitudinous impressions and experiences, thinking and feeling in ways that may complement one another or diverge from one another.

One doesn't just think one morning, "I'm no good. I'm not lovable," and sink into a depression. There are changes of mood, good days and bad days, moments of pure terror and times of reprieve. The important fact is that as poor as my self-image was, and as frightening as the periods of depression were, I refused to give in and simply have a nervous breakdown. I talked to my friends—my patient friends! I prayed, often with the hopeless fear that my prayers were going nowhere. But I prayed. I read the Bible, searching for some words that would assure me God was really there and really caring for me. When things were at their worst, I got dressed and went out—anywhere. Shopping, to the library, to call on a friend, anything—anything to be active, to break the deadly train of thought I couldn't fight at home.

71

In all of this one conviction emerged. Either the Bible was not true or it was. If it were not, then all humanity was in the soup, and my anguish was all one with all the despair of a world going nowhere. If the Bible were true, then all the statements that God cares for His own were true and reliable. Even in my worst moments of anxiety, I could *not* believe that the Bible was nothing but a conglomeration of letters and books written by men who were all wrong, all misled, all deceived. It had the flavor of a unifying spirit greater than the differences of all the varied authors. I had to believe that the Holy Spirit lived and breathed through those pages and that they contained truth I could depend upon.

That conviction was the rock to which I clung when the depression was deep and fears threatened my tenuous grasp on self-control. It had nothing to do with my feelings which were often a mixture of despondency and fear. There were many days I got through ten minutes at a time, reminding myself that my trust was in God and His ability to keep me from falling apart rather than my shaky emotional state.

The recovery was slow but complete with a surprising bonus. The perpetual anxiety and lack of self-acceptance that had plagued me all my life was gone. How tremendous the change was can hardly be realized by those who have gone through life free and untroubled. I had fretted about everything. Walking into a room full of people terrified me—I imagined they were all looking at me with unfriendly criticism.

The Hidden Adversary

I was afraid of the dark, afraid of accidents, afraid of being hurt, afraid of illness. My prayers had always been a litany of fear. "Don't let . . . keep me away from . . . protect me from . . ." That was over.

My attitude toward myself was different. Not that I suddenly decided, "By golly, I'm all right after all! I'm as good as everyone else, and I don't intend to forget it." Not at all. I simply began to think about other people, other things instead of myself. Much of my poor self-image was the outgrowth of intense concentration on myself, a deadly kind of introspection. Since most of us have enough faults and are of unremarkable intellect and abilities, any degree of self-examination will cause even the most equable person to be somewhat low-spirited. One doesn't get over a depression by thinking oneself out of it—that simply forces attention inward and is self-defeating. The best medicine is self-forgetfulness.

That brings up the thorny heart of the issue—disciplining one's thinking is incredibly difficult and demanding. The fatal tendency to let attention and thought slide back to oneself must be fought, and it will take all the reserves of strength there are. At worst, self-absorption can bring one to the brink of despair and death. At best it makes one a bore, like the musician under discussion at a luncheon group of his colleagues. He was neatly disposed of when one of them said, "He's the kind of man who says, 'But that's enough about me. What do *you* think of my voice?'"

CHAPTER SIX

Trapped in a Molasses Vat

"Why don't you talk to a psychologist or professional counselor?" I suggested to my unhappy confidant. "Or at least go and see your pastor. He's a very perceptive person, he ought to be able to help you."

"How?" she asked. "Tell me to pray? I have prayed. Tell me this is my cross to bear? Tell me there are other people worse off than I am, or that it isn't really as bad as it seems? The worst of it all is that I don't see any way out. I could stand almost anything if I knew it would not last forever—but as far as I can tell this is going to last long enough to see me into my grave."

She laughed a little, embarrassed at the melodrama of her last sentence, but I knew she had meant every word. We were sitting in the living room of her home, a pleasant room with French doors instead of windows—very like hundreds of other California bungalows built during the twenties. The room displayed her good taste—soft gray walls and woodwork, a pleasantly faded oriental rug, furniture arranged in conversational groups. It also spoke of a perennial lack of money; everything was just a bit shabby.

A FRIEND'S STORY

I had known Helen for years, a good friendship based on an instinctive liking for one another. Our friendship had just missed being an intimate one, due more to lack of opportunity to be together than choice. Helen had been married to a charming, very good man, the kind who never sets the world on fire but goes on year after year in a responsible though not spectacular job. He was very understanding about her obligations to her family—a semi-invalid mother. Her brother and sister who both lived in another state relied on Helen to care for their mother.

Helen and Sam had one child, a daughter, Valerie, about the age of my own daughter. When Valerie was about twelve Helen's mother came to live with them and unlike many similar situations it worked very well. She was a considerate, perceptive person and got along well with her son-in-law and granddaughter. I don't think that Helen ever considered herself ill-used or a martyr—she managed capably and with humor. When Valerie was about nineteen she married and moved to the East Coast. About that same time the grandmother became much worse; caring for her took most of Helen's day. Eventually she had to be hospitalized and died very shortly.

There wasn't much money and I am sure Helen and Sam bore the greater part of the expenses. All their friends said what a blessing it was that her mother had gone, since life had become such a burden, and that perhaps now Helen and Sam could do some of the things they'd never been able to do. They were planning a trip to Mexico when Sam had a massive coronary and died before the ambulance arrived.

After the first stunning impact wore off Helen began to rally. We'd get together for lunch and sometimes she would break down and weep, but her tears were part of a healthy grief and she was a strong enough Christian to accept death as she had accepted other troubles—as neither final nor defeating. She decided to sell her home, which was far too large for one woman, take an apartment and do some traveling before settling down to some kind of job.

Before any of these plans got under way, Valerie, with two small children and the news that her husband had left her, arrived and that was the final blow.

In the initial flurry of getting Valerie and the children settled, of rearranging and refurbishing bedrooms for them, of giving Valerie what help she could by listening and comforting, Helen had no time to think. Her daughter's needs were her only concern. She was cheerful and reassuring and encouraged Valerie to get a job as soon as possible while she took care of the children.

None of this was very dramatic—as a matter of fact, nothing in her life was very dramatic. Her despair was simply due to the fact that after a lifetime of cheerful caring for other people she was ready for a change, and the prospect of spending the rest of her active life "until I'm in a wheelchair," she said wryly, tied down to routine of housekeeping and caring for children and fixing meals and *always having to be there* was just too much. She was so blue she was practically purple.

After my first timid suggestion that she talk to someone professionally and her reaction to it—with which I was in complete sympathy—we just sat there for a while and stared at each other in silence. For me to have come forth with any glib little clichés or to have quoted a Bible verse or two would have been the most superficial, wounding condescension possible. There are times when there is nothing to say.

The situation Helen was in might have been easily resolved by a more selfish person; someone who could have said, "Don't bring me your problems, my dear. I raised you, now you raise your own children. I'm sorry about the divorce, but you can get an apartment and find a baby-sitter surely. I'd love to see the children, of course, and my Sundays are always free." Helen couldn't do that because she is a loving, caring person. She felt a great deal of empathy for her daughter, who was hurt and needed more than a job and a sitter. She needed someone who loved her, someone to just *be* there.

All this made it even more difficult for Helen to cope with the depression and feeling of frustration she was beginning to have more and more. She couldn't really be herself at all, or express normal fatigue or irritation. At the slightest signal of distress from her, Valerie leaped into action with such anxiety for her mother's feelings, such determination not to be a burden that Helen felt guilty for adding to her burden.

78

Trapped in a Molasses Vat

The afternoon that we talked it out didn't produce any miraculous way out of the problem, but it did set in motion a process that helped Helen overcome her depression and cope satisfactorily with her dilemma.

First of all, she did go to her pastor. Not for some quick answer or handy spiritual panacea, but simply for what encouragement and suggestions he could give. I am her friend, and I could give her my support and understanding, but I couldn't give her advice. She needed some objective advice.

There are two reasons why I believe that except in very uncomplicated, open-and-shut cases friends should play a supportive role but never an advisory one. The first is that very few of us are objective enough when it comes to our friends and family to be fair about our judgment of a situation. My own initial reaction when anyone I care for tells me about an incident that has hurt him is, "How dare they (or he, or she) do this to my friend?" Objectivity just isn't present when we are emotionally involved with people.

The second reason is that the way I would approach a problem is tailored to my temperament and needs, not necessarily to anyone else. What would answer for me might not do at all for Helen; might even cause her more misery and guilt than she already had. Most of us, when we confide in friends, do not really want advice. We know, by a process that is more emotional than rational, that we must make our own decisions; that no one else can impose a tailor-made

79

solution on our lives. What we need desperately is not advice but support—someone who cares about us, someone who is *for* us, someone to give us courage whether we are making right decisions or making mistakes all over the place.

Helen decided that besides talking to her pastor she and her daughter could build a more comfortable situation if they were honest with each other rather than continuing to live in such a strained, overly solicitous atmosphere. She opened the subject very carefully and with immense tact and was surprised and relieved when her daughter said, "Oh, Mother, I've been hoping we could talk like this and just didn't know how to go about it!" They got all their frustrations and irritations and tender areas out in the open, talked them over and worked out a plan for handling problems.

Probably the most constructive plan they came up with was to make arrangements so they wouldn't be together every evening. The daughter was very sympathetic to Helen's need to be alone, to read, eat when she felt in the mood, to not be tied to a routine. She fixed dinner for the children most week nights and took them upstairs. Helen could pursue her own concerns for the evening.

All these methods of easing the situation didn't make it ideal. After all, life isn't ideal either for a divorcee who has to work and support two small children or for a widow. But things were easier, more tolerable, and Helen's depressed periods began to lift. The difference was she was *doing* something about the cause of her depression rather than just remaining passive.

"HOPELESS" CIRCUMSTANCES

Most of the "hopeless" situations we find ourselves in can, like Helen's, be changed for the better even if they cannot be completely done away with. What stops most of us is a kind of mental and emotional lassitude, the result of slogging around the same old track: "I can't change it because . . ." I've felt that way very often myself. The pattern is always the same; I fret about some undesirable circumstance in my life that is caused by factors over which I have no control. I mentally review the situation, considering each factor in turn. No possibility of action presents itself, and in the end, exhausted, I am very, very blue.

The depression itself acts like a drug, slowing down my mental processes and sapping vitality which, in turn, deepens the depression. There have been times when suddenly and surprisingly what seemed so impossible to change has altered radically because of some unexpected development. Or problems have thinned out gradually, and what had once been apparently insoluble finally has disappeared. Most frequently, however, the hard, difficult situations in my life have been modified—not done away with—when I have overcome the tendency to do nothing and made a decision.

When I can't change the circumstances of my life I try to figure out some means of making them more

81

palatable. I came to realize that the vicious cycle of worrying—mentally butting my head against immovable objects, sinking into the blues—was really worse than the very things I worried about. If nothing could be done about my circumstances, I'd have to change my attitude toward them—anything to lighten the picture somewhat.

There is always one immediate reward when I begin to evaluate my attitude toward a problem. Accepting the unalterable rather than fighting it brings a release from tension, even peace, which brightens one's spirits. Once all the energy that had been spent chewing over the problem is released, it can go into more constructive channels. I begin, at that point, to consider some of the possibilities for making my situation more tolerable. There are *always* some ways of coping with a disagreeable fact in life; but they will never become apparent until the fact itself is accepted.

Molly Ringer, a dear friend for many years, follows this principle in her own life. She has been a diabetic all her adult life and during the past two years has gradually lost her vision. As an active, outgoing woman the frustration of living in perpetual darkness and being increasingly limited in what she can do could have made her bitter and fretful. Instead, she decided that since there was nothing she could do to change her situation she would accept it and enjoy everything she could without worrying over the pleasures now impossible.

She is a Christian with a deep commitment to

Christ, which is the source of her strength; but there's a great deal of self-discipline and common sense involved too. Obviously, to handle this heartbreaking problem with such maturity would not have been possible if Molly hadn't handled other, smaller problems in the same way. One arrives at the ability to cope with hard places in life by coping with each day's difficulties responsibly, one step at a time. There is no such thing as instantaneous maturity. It has to grow slowly.

Molly is not depressed, though she must have periods of being blue; but neither is her cheerfulness the assumed "brave-little-woman" pose which is so nauseating. If there is anything that is worse than the blues, it's the martyred saint syndrome, which indicates that underneath a syrupy exterior the disease of resentment and frustration is still raging. The chronically blue person who tells all his friends about his hopeless problem is matched by the chronically brave sufferer who compels attention by being showily forbearing. One must fight the temptation to dramatize one's troubles; it's the first thought that comes when one accepts the inevitable. "Well," the thought leaps to mind, "now everyone will see how spiritual I really am."

Don't do it. It will alienate more people than the most vociferous complaints and is ruinous to the character besides. Somehow being a martyred saint bleeds away all humor and balance from those who play that part. You see, both the one who inflicts her low spirits on others and the one who uses her problem as a means of dramatizing her virtues are alike in one respect: They see themselves as the center of the stage, always. The slightest touch of humor would explode such pretensions at once. There are countless others living with their particular troubles; with neither complaint nor ostentation. Whatever one's situation is, it is certainly not unique and very likely not the worst. Reminding oneself of that from time to time will do wonders to overcome any subtle tendencies toward self-dramatization.

IMPOSSIBLE PEOPLE

While situations might change, however, it is only too true that the impossible people in our lives don't. Everyone has, at some time, played one of two roles— either as the victim of an "impossible" person or as highly objectionable himself. For those readers who suspect they may be in the second category there will be a few words at the end of the chapter.

If there is someone in your life whose very voice on the phone or at the door can send your spirits plummeting, then read on. There may be something constructive one can do, however insoluble the problem seems.

First of all, there is a great deal of fuzzy thinking among Christians about our obligations to such people. We've come to believe that being Christian means being "nice" or pretending we like everyone; or even agreeing with everyone, no matter how disagreeable or how repellant their attitudes. We feel that to take issue with anyone means we have just rejected him, so we go about smoothing things over, covering up disagreements with a surface smoothness which hardly hides the lumps underneath. I believe that this is not particularly Christian. Rather, it is wrong and certainly self-defeating. It provokes more problems than it solves.

One result of such wishy-washy "niceness" is that the frustration it produces deepens into depression. There is no way out of such dejection unless the pseudo-Christian point of view that says we've always got to be nice no matter what is abandoned. Being nice to people who don't bother to be nice themselves merely encourages them in their tyranny. It works so well, why change?

Still, one doesn't want to go through life in a series of pitched battles; there are some times when the issue at stake isn't important enough to warrant a fight. That is a good principle for most human relationships, but when the impossible person is involved, it doesn't apply. First of all, there is one thing all these impossible people have in common, whether a difficult husband or encroaching neighbor or the freeloader at the next desk. They want *everything* their own way. There is no way on earth to get along with these people short of continually giving in to them, and that doesn't make them any pleasanter. It only convinces them there's no reason at all why they should ever be thwarted.

The world is full of wives married to such men, who

have tried for years to please them, and who always think, "If just this once he's happy, then perhaps he'll be easier to get along with." He won't. No wonder these women are low spirited and always under it a little. They are on a treadmill going nowhere. What puzzles me is how the idea that giving in to selfish, arrogant people is Christian ever got started. It's about as effective as giving in to the bank robber on the theory that if he's given no trouble this time, he'll never do it again.

There's another reason behind the passivity many of us exhibit in our relationships. We all hate unpleasantness. Raised voices and ugly words can make cowards out of most of us. It's easier, we feel, to smooth over an embarrassing social situation than to subject those around to a painful scene; easier even to be conciliatory and soothing when there are no onlookers. Easier far on the nerves.

There are cases where this is undoubtedly so. A friend married to a man who occasionally grows unreasonable and loses his temper has developed great expertise in both calming her husband and saving the social situation. She knows that eventually he will be sorry and humbled, loathing himself for his excesses of temper; making him defensive about it doesn't help at all. He's an intelligent man and realizes very well the ugliness of his temper. His wife makes it easier for him to try to control himself by remaining cool than she would if she tore into him every time he flew off the handle.

Trapped in a Molasses Vat

THE HIGHEST CHRISTIAN LOVE

There is a difference, however, between occasional lapses and the person who habitually trades on the good taste and restraint of everyone around him, counting on their courtesy to let him get by with rudeness or selfishness. I just don't believe it is particularly helpful —or Christian—to let these petty tyrants go on year after year congratulating themselves that they are above the conventions everyone else observes.

Those who advocate excusing the bad behavior of the impossible person on the grounds that it is the Christian thing to do usually quote from the Sermon on the Mount: "You have heard that it used to be said 'An eye for an eye and a tooth for a tooth,' but I tell you, don't resist the man who wants to harm you. If a man hits your right cheek, turn the other one to him as well. If a man wants to sue you for your coat, let him have it and your overcoat as well. If anybody forces you to go a mile with him, do more—go two miles with him. Give to the man who asks anything from you, and don't turn away from the man who wants to borrow."

Jesus then concluded with the famous instructions about loving our enemies, on the basis that God loves *His* enemies—were we not all in that category one time or another? And furthermore, that He sheds His blessings on the just and unjust alike. We are not to discriminate.

Well and good. We have to consider what Jesus said in the light of His total teaching, which includes the command to treat other people exactly as we

would like to be treated by them—the Golden Rule—
with somewhat cryptic advice not to give holy things to
dogs nor throw pearls before pigs lest they trample
them underfoot, turn and attack us; and with His
teaching that if a brother wrongs any one of us, the
thing to do is go and have it out with him. If he refuses to listen, then take one or two others as witnesses
and try again; and if he still refuses, bring the matter
before the church. We also have to remember that He
never minced words when it came to talking to people
about their sins. He made it plain that there is forgiveness, but He never ignored the distinction between
right and wrong.

The thread that draws these seemingly opposing
statements together seems to me to be that of motive.
Jesus expects us to be motivated by a desire to obey
God. Everything we have—the capacity to love, to
forgive, to reach out to others—we have because God
gave it to us. Thus, we forgive because we are for-
given, and we love because we are loved—by God.

Now the one thing His love does not do is pretend
that we're all right just the way we are. He *accepts* us
as we are—that is the rock-bottom assurance we all
rely on. But He's not pleased with our spiritual grub-
biness, our shabby pretense of rectitude; the very reason Christ came was to make it possible for us to be
delivered from all that makes us the poor things we are
when left to ourselves. God's love is directed to making
us what He designed us to be, what we could never be
on our own. He intends to free us from all that inhibits

our growth as real persons, and there is no pretense that we're all right just as we are. Some of the sternest things Jesus said were said in order to strip away the defenses men gather around themselves in order to avoid facing their need to change.

The highest Christian love, therefore, follows that pattern. It does *not* excuse all moral and ethical failures, overlook all rudeness and selfishness on the basis that Christians ought to think well of one another. Both rudeness and selfishness, though they seem such small social sins compared with, say, embezzlement, are really merely minute versions of gargantuan sins. They say in social exchange what armed robbery says in violence—that the one who lives that way wants what he wants regardless of what he does to others to get it.

Therefore, it seems to me that the best Christian attitude to take when we are faced with an impossible person is that we will go the second mile—turn the other cheek—but never in a spirit of capitulation. I say this knowing that I have very seldom been able to live up to my own words. I have—just as all of you have done the easiest thing—often put up with unpardonable rudeness out of fear of making a scene, refused to stand for what I really believed because it would have meant a fight, remained silent when I should have spoken because it would have been socially gauche. I'm ashamed of it, and am trying a different way of living.

It is difficult because it's always hard to be honest,

and in the Christian world it's sometimes even more so than in the average secular crowd. We've made such a phony virtue out of being agreeable, as if merely being pleasant were real Christian love. It's time to change, because all the smiling and agreeing and refusing to face differences honestly, refusing to speak up when someone is behaving abominably just has not worked. You see, it never was genuine at all. The smiling compliance was only for the moment. Later most of our criticism and all the resentment and hurt and anger came out; gossip about others isn't always out of sheer malice, it may be out of wounded feelings and anger.

I have concluded that some people are impossible precisely because no one has ever compelled them to face themselves as they are. They can always rationalize temper or laziness or selfishness because it is never called by name. The kind of honesty that is called for here is, of course, an honesty wrapped in love. I have accepted some very critical assessments about myself from time to time because the one doing the talking really loved me, and I knew it. Genuine love, so different from the shallow good will we call "love," means that any criticism or reproof we offer will be done tactfully and with sensitivity. It's a far cry from the crudeness so typical of the person who proclaims, before she delivers her broadsides, "I'm very honest," or, "Now, I believe in being frank about these things." Honesty is only helpful so long as it is linked with love.

Trapped in a Molasses Vat

THE LIMPET AND WHAT TO DO

I've left until last the most treacherous of all dilemmas with impossible people—those meek, helpless, ineffectual persons who cling like limpets and from whom you cannot walk away because they need you so much. All we know of pity and forbearance prevents us from freeing ourselves, and the irritation and frustration that result are always mixed with a kind of helplessness. Such people are so pitiful that to cast them off would, we instinctively feel, make us monsters.

After years of watching how these helpless clingers operate, both in my life and in the lives of others, I have concluded that they have been grossly misjudged. They are strong, very strong. Strong enough to manipulate those far better and more intelligent and more capable than they are; all that seeming weakness is an illusion. By appearing so helpless and defenseless they worm their way into the lives of their victims and before long are running the whole show.

That sounds very melodramatic, but the truth often is rather like an overdone thriller, which is why we have become enmeshed in situations before we know it—it's hard to believe that this dear little woman, so solicitous, so timid, so fearful of offending, could be other than just what she seems.

Some years ago a friend of mine was the target of just such a helpless, weak woman. At first it was all so innocuous—we were all members of the same group in a large church, and poor Annie was so shy and in need

91

of friendship that we went out of our way to be kind to her. She, apparently with unerring accuracy, picked my friend as her target, for Helen is the kindest and most patient of women. Annie had confided the hardships of her life to us—an unsympathetic husband who, though he made a good salary, kept her on a pittance; who made no secret of his affairs with other women, and (here her voice always sank) *drank*.

She began phoning Helen when she was especially distraught, and the phone calls grew more and more frequent and at the same time longer, so that Helen spent hours each week—sometimes every day—on the phone. After a time it became apparent that Annie, in spite of the fact that she always said, "but what shall I *do?*" did not have any intention of doing anything. She was an abominable housekeeper and still worse cook, which, she said, was out of discouragement. Why try to keep a clean house for a husband who was never home? Why cook good meals when she might end up eating them alone? To all suggestions that she improve in these areas, for her own benefit and comfort if not her husband's, she responded, "Oh, what's the use? God knows I'd do anything if he would appreciate it, but he won't. You just don't understand the way he is."

The stories began to be repetitious, the excuses for her slovenliness rather thin, and a certain self-pitying whine was evident. Annie threw out broad hints about how lonely she was on Sundays, how she'd go to this function or that one if only someone would just pick her up. "You don't know how frightening it is to have to drive somewhere alone at night. Of course you've got a husband who takes you places so you couldn't possibly know what it's like to be all alone night after night" . . . and on and on.

Helen was beginning to feel trapped. It was difficult to go anywhere or do anything without a prior call from Annie, plaintively wondering if she'd be a bother; of course, if it was too much trouble . . . Finally, after a lot of thinking and a great deal of prayer, Helen went to Annie and told her she felt the conversations were not helpful to Annie, were devastating to her and should stop. She was kind and gentle and considerate, but honest. She pointed out that whatever Annie's situation was, no one could change it but herself or her husband, and if he wasn't willing to try, then she must either accept him and the life she led with him or do something herself to change it. There was a great deal more she said, but none of it mattered. At the first sentence Annie was hurt; then outraged; then unjustly accused. She closed the episode by saying, with the air of Saint Joan at the stake, "You don't need to say any more. I can see what it is. You don't want to be bothered with me. I should have known all that Christian love and friendship was just a fake. Friendship! There certainly hasn't been much of it shown to me. I'll just go on alone as I always have. No one really cares when you're helpless." Helen was speechless with sheer frustration and then, deciding that Annie was impervious to anything more she might say,

93

left. What happened to Annie I do not know except that she moved on to another group and a few months later I heard that several of the women in that group were afraid to answer their phone for fear it would be Annie again.

Those terribly weak ones who, like Annie, engulf their victims with their own helplessness, are not really helpless at all. They have chosen weakness as a means of achieving their goal which is to make someone—everyone—carry their responsibilities. They often succeed, as anyone who has gotten enmeshed will testify.

There *is* a Christian point of view about this problem, and it is found in a letter Paul wrote to the Galatians. A very sound piece of advice: Paul wrote, in the last chapter of the letter, that Christians should help each other keep on the right track, correcting the one who is offside but not with any feeling of superiority. In that context he said, "Carry each other's burdens." He then went on to warn against pride and advised his readers to be able to assess the value of their own work. In that context he said, "For every man must 'shoulder his own pack.'" What he was saying in essence was that we must care for each other, be honest about each other's failings and do all we can to help each man stay on the right track—in that sense, we do bear each other's burdens. We empathize, we pray, we support. But we do *not* do for another what he ought to do for himself. At the point of his own responsibility, each man "carries his own pack." There are far too many Christians going about with a burden of depression because they are trying to help someone who won't be helped. All the hopelessness and the frustration of a constant irritant is enough to drain the joy out of life, and it's in the wrong cause. There's no virtue in permitting anyone to become a human leech. Get the burden off your back—gently if possible, kindly, tactfully—but firmly. It's not unchristian, and you may be saving two lives—his and yours.

Remember that I am talking about freeing yourself from people who use the sympathy and help they get from others as a means of avoiding their own responsibilities. There are, on the other hand, those whose burdens really are too heavy for them to bear without the support and encouragement of friends. I'm not advocating a wholesale casting off of all concern and help for other people. I am talking about the discernment to tell which are the ones who genuinely need support and friendship and which are the ones who use their weakness as a weapon to pass their responsibilities on to someone else. It's a pity one can't make blanket rules to cover all situations, but rules governing human relationships are a poor substitute for love, concern and sensitivity. If there is any prayer suitable for all of us in getting along with difficult people it's the prayer for discernment.

THE CLINGING YOU

One last word about impossible people. It's unrealistic to expect that any of us can go through life without someone in a close relationship who is somewhere in the category from "touchy" to "utterly impossible." It may be a son or a daughter or close relative or a friend of long standing whose claims on one's friendship can't be ignored. Some of these people may be going through temporary periods of emotional stress and need, as never before, all the affirmation we can give them. And certainly anyone who has had teen-agers knows that *they* need to be loved the most when they deserve it the least. For times such as this there are two things to be done. First, prayer. Prayer for the person, and prayer for oneself—for strength and patience and fortitude. Secondly, someone to talk to, someone objective, who won't talk and who can give sound, practical help. That will in most cases be a trained counselor or minister.

We all are faced with impossible people from time to time. Some may fall to our lot the way rain falls on the just and the unjust alike. We need to learn how to cope with them gracefully and, if possible, to their good. Others may be helped best by being gently but firmly set on their own two feet. We need to pray for the wisdom to know one from the other.

If, on the other hand, *you* are sunk in self-pity and the blues because you find your friends unsympathetic, unwilling to listen to your troubles, it may be that *you* need to stop clinging. There's a very fine line between the perfectly normal need we all have to confide in someone, to seek encouragement and support, and obsessive leaning on others. You can tell when you are in danger of becoming an impossible person in that way by the fact that you'll find friends less available than they used to be.

It's perfectly legitimate to talk over your troubles with friends, but if it's become a habit and you're forever telling the same old story, you're in danger. If talking has become your method of temporary release rather than action, which you could take but don't—you're in even greater danger.

Self-pity will only make things worse. No matter how sad and hopeless your situation is, you can complain to others only so long before they begin to grow impatient. It's not that people are hard-hearted. It's just that they have only so much emotional energy to spend in sympathy, and you can get to the end of it. Only God is limitless in His compassion and patience. Complain to Him—loudly, vociferously, not in the semi-liturgical language most of us think proper for prayer, but honestly. You might as well; He knows how you feel anyway. Once you are honest with God, He can begin to help you. I have no idea how the help will come because He can't be confined by our little patterns. Some new circumstance may arise which changes the whole situation. Nothing but your attitude and ability to cope with life may change. But help will come.

CHAPTER SEVEN

They'll Be Sorry

The word "depressed" brings to mind most frequently a mental picture of someone with a downcast expression just sitting—doing nothing. To be depressed is often, we assume, to be passive.

MASK FOR ANGER

There is a kind of depression that masks hostility, however, and it is the farthest remove from passivity. Regardless of the seeming lethargy, the failing voice or the suffused eyes, those whose low spirits are a cover for hostility are not as helpless as they seem. Their mopishness is used as a weapon, though they may not be conscious of what they are doing. We are prone to conceal from ourselves what our real motives are, and it is easy indeed to hide one's fury and rage behind a mask of depression. That very depression can then be used to punish others. It's better than kicking and scratching, and there's very little defense against it.

One woman I knew made a whole group of friends miserable by her moods, which ranged from slightly blue to deeply depressed. One friend, after a ghastly

99

evening spent with her, said to me thoughtfully, "You know, her depression is really frozen rage." At first this sounded unlikely to me, but then I remembered how often the woman we were discussing had betrayed her resentment toward others. She was unhappy; why should others be so carefree and lighthearted?

Since I had gone through a period of depression in my own life, I began to look back to see how much hostility had been part of my own unhappiness. Honesty compelled me to admit what I could not have faced at the time I was in the middle of it. There was a great deal of anger hidden by the dejection. In fact, much of my trouble was the accumulation of hostility over a number of years and that, in turn, was the result of my unwillingness to settle with the realities of life.

First of all, there was the fact that my marriage (like all marriages) wasn't absolutely idyllic. There were areas of sensitivity which we handled by tiptoeing around them. There were the usual adjustments imperfectly made, and my disgruntlement at having to make them at all. In addition to that, and probably far more serious, was the turmoil inside me that was the result of discovering that God doesn't solve all the problems, take away all the obstacles, answer all my prayers like some spiritual sugar daddy.

This last was the most frustrating and difficult to accept because, like so many Christians today, I was surrounded by untroubled people who believed implicitly that the truly "spiritual" Christian is delivered

100

from all the problems and tragedies of life. Their testimonies were always glowing accounts of miraculous cures, financial success and personal victory over sin.

Now, even though I was beginning to be knowledgeable enough about the Bible to know that this was not a true picture of the way God works in our lives, still —there they were, so confident, so sure of themselves and their position, so free (apparently) of any doubts or conflicts or unsolvable problems. Why wasn't my life like that? When I wrote a bit about that fight with real depression in Chapter Five, I didn't mention the hostility, but it was certainly there. One never can tell things without glossing over enormously complicated sequences of events, compressing into a sentence or two experiences that had many aspects, and necessarily compartmentalizing that which was complex and layered and composed of many overlapping emotions. Sometimes as I recall that period of life, one aspect stands out in my memory, sometimes another— but the hostility was part of it, though I could not have admitted it.

I was angry at God, fundamentally, because life wasn't perfect, and I wasn't perfect, and yet there were so many around me who insisted with infuriating complacency that it was and they were. I don't mean to say that they were responsible for my particular bout of depression—but they were part of the picture.

WHOSE FAULT?

It seems to me that many of us, myself included, think like this: When we love someone we want to make

101

them happy; and we think we make people happy by giving them all the good things they ask for and taking away anything that interferes with their happiness. Therefore if God loves me, He wants to make me happy and will give me the desires of my heart and certainly remove anything which is less than perfect. We don't think this out step by step, of course, but underneath our conscious thinking lies this highly emotional, unthinking analysis of what God is like and how He works. Part of our tendency to equate the good life with the happy life may arise from the American assumption that there is nothing our expertise can't solve, and when there are no problems we are bound to be happy.

The woman I wrote about at the beginning of the chapter fell into that category. She wasn't as pretty as she wanted to be, not as outgoing or sure of herself as she would have liked to be, and none of her friends were able to give her enough attention to assure her that she was really worthwhile. Because of her own inability to accept herself as she was, she needed an inordinate amount of reassurance from others; and, of course, didn't get it. The result was a gigantic case of the sulks, which is what that kind of depression often is. She hated God for not making her different; she hated her friends for not loving her as much as she wanted them to; and she punished everybody by being impossible.

Her glum little face and showy silences were meant to make others uncomfortable. She was saying to them, "See what you've done to me? See how miserable you make me? I'm pathetic and unhappy, and it's all your fault."

The obvious step to take in these days when everything that goes wrong is attributed to psychological causes would have been to go for help, but it was a long time before the woman I speak of was willing to do so. She would never have gone, no doubt, but for the fact that one by one her friends became tired of her bad behavior and dropped her. As long as there was someone around she could punish, she avoided facing her problem honestly. Finally, with no object for her hostility available, she did see a psychiatrist and, after a lengthy period of counseling, began to improve. She's much happier now than she would ever have thought possible. There are old friendships fractured beyond repair, of course; they were part of the price she paid for her illness. But she's made new ones and is handling her situation in life very well.

This is not a story of magic cures. Like many of us, she will always fight the temptation to blame someone —her parents, her friends, her husband, God—when things go wrong. But she's grown up enough now to reject that and to accept the fact that in this life nothing is ever totally perfect. It's the same lesson I had to learn, and when I add up the benefits from it I can say that the depression was worth it.

THE VICIOUS CYCLE

Of the people I've known fairly well who have suffered prolonged bouts of depression, all have admitted to deep feelings of anger. Sometimes the admission did not come until the worst of the depression was over, and usually after some counseling. Many of these people were Christians, and they seemed to have just as tough a time conquering their problems as anyone else. Two of them had far more trouble even facing the problem *because* of their Christianity than they would have had without it. Why? Why should anyone in touch with the author of life and happiness and hope be subject to hostility and depression?

Perhaps some of the attitudes that have come to be common among evangelicals may be responsible for our troubles. And these attitudes are not found in the Bible; they are something we have added. They arise out of a profound misunderstanding of the gospel, and are partly the product of the culture in which we live. As we mentioned before, it's a problem-solving culture.

The Christian version, a vulgarized form of the faith, assumes that not only does God solve all our problems and sweep away all difficulties, He gives us what is often referred to as "the victorious life"—by which is meant a kind of spiritual euphoria so that nothing distresses us. I've heard glowing testimonies about the peace and joy one feels in the most agonizing circumstances—a death in the family, for instance, or a long and debilitating illness. All that is true, of course. I've known that peace and joy many times— at the grave of our nine-year-old daughter, the first of many deaths in my family. But it is *not* true that such

104

peace and joy are there instead of sorrow and loneliness and the anguish of loss. They are there *with* all the human emotions we all have, not instead of them.

Christians who believe that Christ's promise of peace and joy for his people meant they would never suffer or be unhappy again are pathetically dependent on feelings, upon the absence of ordinary human emotions under stress and trouble, for their spiritual security. I heard that kind of testimony for many years, and it didn't match my experience.

It was a relief, therefore, to discover how very little the Bible has to say about feelings. True, joy is mentioned a great deal in the New Testament, but since it is mentioned in connection with persecution and suffering for the sake of the gospel, it is obviously not the same as the happiness we so firmly believe is our greatest good.

Most of us, when we become Christians, transfer our purely secular and quite unfounded concept of happiness as the greatest good over to our Christian lives and superimpose it on what we read in the Bible. It's not a conscious process, just a very naïve and unthinking assumption.

When this childish kind of Christianity bumps up against the real world, as it inevitably must for all of us, we become angry like spoiled children screaming when they can't have their own way. Anger, however, is a no-no. The same simplistic, unrealistic view of Christianity which says that good Christians are rewarded by being happy all the time also says that all

105

negative emotions are bad. If you have them, you aren't being good, and if you aren't good, you certainly won't be happy.

The usual result is that we refuse to face our negative and unwanted emotions and try to pretend they're not there at all. Anger so smothered, so repressed, surfaces again, as it must, but in a new form—depression. The vicious cycle is complete, and not only complete but reinforced by the Christian society many of us live in. We don't dare face our anger because it's so unchristian, so of course we can't admit to anyone that it's there—we have to be "victorious Christians" in order to be acceptable to our peers. The attempt to be happy and serene and untroubled at all times is quite a strain, which deepens the hostility burbling around under the surface, and when it finally breaks out in its disguised form of depression, the trouble is compounded.

THE FALLACY OF "VICTORIOUS" CHRISTIANS

Not only is any hostility unacceptable in this superficial little scheme of Christian living, but depression is also considered a sign of unspirituality. The poor soul who finds himself in the grip of an emotion so damaging to his image as a good Christian often thinks, in his desperation, that he needs spiritual help. There must be something wrong with his relationship with Christ for him to be so miserable. It's about as logical an assumption as thinking that reading a good devotional book will mend a broken leg. But then Christians, like the rest of the world, are seldom logical.

They'll Be Sorry

The Church, in such a situation, is contributing to the illness of its people rather than helping them to become well. We have far too many sincere, earnest Christians suffering from depression rooted in hostility. We need to correct the basic errors in our thinking that have helped to make this a problem.

The first is, of course, the assumption that being a Christian means one will always be happy and trouble-free. Wherever this crops up, demand authentification. Where does the Bible say that? Where are the words, in black and white, that tell us we have a right to expect to be perpetually happy? They aren't there, and the sooner we face that fact, the happier we'll be. That sounds contradictory, but it isn't. There is a genuine happiness that is not the result of having all possible distress removed from life but from being at peace with the life God has given us. Happiness is probably not a good word—joy would be more like it. We can be serene at the center of our lives even though the surface may be troubled at times, sorrowful at times, or subject to irritation and fatigue. We can accept these disturbances because they have nothing to do with our real destiny and are temporary, if distressing, problems. But as long as we expect to be perpetually free of any negative emotions, we're in trouble.

The hostility we've been taught by so many Christians is very bad but not half as damaging as the pretense that it's not there at all. You can begin to cope with a condition when you face the fact that it exists, and not until then. If most of us have learned to conceal our hostility toward other people because it doesn't fit the image of the spiritual Christian, how much more must we deny even to ourselves our feelings of hostility toward God. That was what I was doing during that frightening period when depression threatened to become a nervous breakdown. All the frustration and anxiety and anger I felt at the circumstances of my life coalesced in a profound anger at God.

The climax of that struggle came with the illness and death of our daughter, Carole Ann. She was not quite ten, a merry, lighthearted little girl whose sense of humor never failed; not even during the dreary months of her illness as she grew weaker and slipped into helplessness. As I watched her, took her to the doctor, did my housework, carried on some sort of show of everyday living, my inner life was a battleground. I did my vacuuming while raging at God. I cooked the meals as I implored Him to make Carole Ann well again. I went to church and listened to the sermons and found myself flinging questions at God the whole time.

There came a time when, exhausted by the battle, I simply gave in and said, "All right, God, I don't understand it at all and it hurts like hell, but if you are determined to take Carole Ann, then I accept your will." It was certainly not a victory, more an unconditional surrender, but it meant an end to the struggle. And, of course, I was surrounded by a Christian community which both helped and hindered me.

Those friends who gave me their support and sympathy without sermonizing or trying to buck me up with little homilies were a source of immense help. There were others who meant well (deadly but accurate description) and in their very determination to help me made life very difficult. They were those whose faith had come to be an assumption that nothing very bad would ever happen to a Christian because Jesus came to make us victorious people; but sad things, such as the death of Carole Ann, did obviously happen. The only way they could account for such events in the life of a believer was to assure me that a close relationship with Jesus Christ delivered one from the *anguish* ordinary secular people suffered. Real Christians were so triumphant in their faith in God that nothing could hurt them.

I tried awfully hard to believe that, in spite of the fact that there were many other friends who warned against such a superficial view of the tragedies of life. The anger I had felt toward God went underground at that time. I honestly thought it had gone. The peace and joy I knew was genuine, but life is never static, and that buried hostility would have to be dealt with.

A year later when we were transferred to a midwestern city and I went through the pangs of homesickness and loneliness, quivering in every nerve at being uprooted, the hostility burst out with a vengeance —this time as depression. It was, though I did not admit it, a weapon. God was too much for me to fight, and I hid even from myself the still simmering hostility toward him. But there was my husband, a legitimate target for my fury. He had insisted on making the move in spite of all my opposition; he was untroubled by having cut all our ties, and I was miserable.

In the end my misery and inability to cope with life forced him to agree to move back to California. How easily we can deceive ourselves! I would have been unbelieving and hurt if anyone had told me then that all that depression, the sickness that was frightening me nearly out of my mind, was my weapon against my husband; and that even punishing him for my misery was a substitute for fighting God.

The recovery was slow and agonizing and moving home did not turn the trick. It took me several years to climb completely out of that morass, and it was not until years later that I could look back and admit what the real circumstances had been. The wonder is that in spite of my hostility toward God I got the help from Him I needed. It was, as anyone who has ever been depressed will know, very, very slow and difficult.

But all the time I was learning to face—and thus to cope with—anger and frustration and the depression they produced, I was thinking through my Christian faith and coming to a more realistic view of what God is doing with us.

I don't know how much depression on the part of secular people is caused by anger, but I would hazard a guess it is about the same problem it is among Christians. That sounds like heresy (Christians, obviously, ought to be better able to cope with life than anyone else), but I believe it is true. And I think the main

110

cause is, as I said, our silly and shallow idea that Christ came to make us happy. Even as we mouth the words, "He died for our sins," we are often adding under our breath, "and everything else that might interfere with our happiness." When difficulties come in the lives of people who really believe that kind of gospel, the natural response is fury, masked as self-hatred or despair.

The only way to combat that dangerous distortion of the truth is to go back to a very careful, serious reading of the Bible. We will find that all the hard, wounding experiences of life are calmly accepted as being inevitable and that the Christian also faces additional hardships because of his faith. However, the picture is not all gloom and darkness. We are promised help when we need it. Paul, a most practical man, writing of the difficulties of living the Christian life in pagan Rome, summed it up this way: "This doesn't mean, of course, that we have only a hope of future joys—we can be full of joy here and now even in our trials and troubles. Taken in the right spirit these very things will give us patient endurance; this in turn will develop a mature character, and a character of this sort produces a steady hope, a hope that will never disappoint us."

CHAPTER EIGHT

Ghosts in the House

In this day of blatant self-exposure, when it's fashionable to discuss one's most intimate thoughts and feelings especially when couched in the language of psychology, there is still one emotion most of us are ashamed of. We may admit to most of the negative feelings we all have, but we shrink from revealing this one, perhaps because it's been impressed upon all of us so thoroughly that the emotion itself is somehow disgraceful.

You've probably already guessed what it is—and you're right. Fear, that most unpleasant of sensations which churns the stomach and flutters the diaphragm and imparts a smothering sensation as well as making hands icy and feet leaden. The worst of it is that because the very admission is so humbling, we hate to admit we are afraid even to ourselves.

And that is why when under the surface of much of the depression suffered by so many people today fear lies coiled like a tiny snake. Of course, when one thinks of the world in which we live, fear seems not only quite logical but inevitable. There are so many things to be afraid of, and with the instant communication that keeps us informed of what is happening all over the world, we have to know about them all. Sometimes it seems an intolerable burden to be aware of so much. With that awareness goes the certainty that wars and political upheavals in Europe and Asia and Africa will have their effects in our lives also. We are not merely moved with compassion or pity or horror but weighted down with fear. And, for most of us, the fear is compounded by the frustrating knowledge that we can't do anything about these distant but threatening events. That in itself can produce quite a somber cast over one's spirits.

More immediate, however, is the news about one's own city and neighborhood. From the riots and mass violence of the sixties to highjackings and outbursts of apparently meaningless violence on the part of individuals who go on shooting sprees, life suddenly seems fraught with danger. People who once walked their dogs at night without a thought of possible harm now not only do not venture out at night, but refuse to open the door to anyone knocking after dark.

These are just general fears to which we are all, to some extent, subject. We live in a culture that has become unpredictable and dangerous, and this fact alone has made us all a little fearful. A kind of climate of general, unspecified anxiety prevails, and it's very difficult not to be affected. That kind of fear isn't so difficult to admit, but it produces a sensitivity that makes us vulnerable in many other areas, and in

114

those realms it's not so easy to say, "I'm afraid." In fact, the very admission that one is afraid of another world war or a nuclear holocaust or a world-wide depression or being mugged after dark or any of the prevailing menaces can become an excuse for admitting our own more personal fears.

FEAR OF FAILURE

We can hide, even from ourselves, our real terrors by setting up substitutes and more-acceptable bogeymen. I've done it often enough myself to know how it works, and I suspect I am not alone. Fear of failure was my particular ghost, and I avoided risking it by simply refusing to take on responsibilities. "I'd love to help you out," I'd say when someone asked me to take an office in women's work, for instance, "but right now I'm too tied up with obligations to take on anything else." I never said what those obligations were because they were nothing more than the household jobs nearly every woman handles.

I never minded teaching Sunday school or serving as program chairman or writing a play for the monthly party—these were areas in which I moved with comfort. But any job that required organizational ability frightened me to death, so I successfully slid out of those responsibilities until the day I was asked to be president of our church's Women's Association. Fresh out of excuses, I said I would take the job if my husband consented, feeling sure he would tell me I had enough to do at home without getting involved in any-

115

thing else. To my surprise and horror he assured me he thought it my duty to accept the job, and I was left without a rag of excuse. I took the job.

Those two years broke me of the habit of hiding my own fear of failure behind a facade, and taught me some lessons I should have learned years before. I learned to plan ahead, to think a project through and break it down into segments small enough to be handled. I learned how to work with other people in a team effort and how to run a meeting so that everything gets done and no one feels cheated out of a chance to speak and the meeting still finishes on time. Most important of all, I learned that failure isn't the end of everything. Sometimes I forgot things or didn't handle them as well as I might have, and I discovered that admitting my ineptness wasn't so painful as it once would have been and no one held it against me.

For some, the fear of failure is hidden away so deeply that it is never rooted out. One woman never had children, though her husband wanted a family. She said the world was too dangerous and depraved to bring children into, but in a moment of frankness she admitted to me that she was really afraid of childbirth. Her mother had told her horrible tales of her experiences giving birth to children, and she was so terrified of being hurt physically—perhaps dying—that she could not face pregnancy. The sad thing is that most of the time she really believed the story about a too-dangerous world. After having told me about her fears of childbirth she retreated so precipitately from it that she couldn't even accept the fact that we had talked about it—our friendship was over. It was easier to keep up with the pretense without being forced to remember that there was one woman who knew the truth.

I don't want to make fun of a very real threat or treat anxieties as if they were nothing, but I must admit that I've known far too many men locked into jobs they hated but were afraid to change simply out of the fear of failure. It's an odd thing about that horror of failing, too, because it exists in spite of all the lip service we give to persistence which is simply the quality that enables one to go on and try again. No one talks about persisting in success—it is only needed where there has been failure. We love stories about inventors who succeeded at last after having failed many times, as Thomas Edison's life testifies. *The Little Train that Could* was a favorite story of my childhood and probably yours—but perhaps we wrote it off as a pleasant fairy tale while real life, regretfully, was not like that. Still, persistence is greatly admired—but not the failure that enables it to be demonstrated.

PEOPLE AND LONELINESS

The thought of failing in business or in a profession is dreadful enough, but even worse is the haunting fear of failing in human relationships. I've known a few uncomplicated, breezy souls who galloped through life with the happy certainty that everyone loved them.

117

They never skulked outside the door of a crowded room, afraid to enter and be the focus of possibly unfriendly or (far worse) indifferent eyes. They never felt as they drew near a group of friends that it was a tight, exclusive little group with no welcome for them. But the rest of us—most of us, I'm sure—have suffered moments of acute anxiety rooted in the fear of not being accepted, of failing *as a person*. The fears may have been groundless; the group of friends delighted to see us, the roomful of people not inimical and all our fancied doubts needless. But the fear itself is very real, and we need to have a way of coping with it.

That particular fear, by the way, seems always to be accompanied by, or followed by, a very low state of mind. The most depressed woman I ever knew was so afraid of not being accepted that she had prickles all over her, rather like a hedgehog. She repelled others before they could repel her. Her behavior at times was very aggravating, almost as if she wanted to prove to herself that no one would put up with her.

When one is as deeply bound up as that in self-doubt and determined to prove failure in human relationships, the only thing to do is go at once to a good, professional counselor. But that is extreme, and there are many who, by coping with these anxieties now can avoid the professional psychologist or psychiatrist in the future.

But before we talk about handling the problem, there are two other huge, threatening clouds of fear that ought to be mentioned: fear of loneliness and fear of the future.

Ghosts in the House

Loneliness is so unbearable to most of us that one is tempted to simply describe it in heartrending terms and let it go at that. What can be done for the solitary person who just can't seem to attract friends? Everything I am going to say will sound contradictory, but it's the truth as I've seen it work out in my life and the lives of others.

First of all, the people who attract me and appear desirable as friends are (1) interested in life—in art, or music, or working with underprivileged children, or learning to make pottery—whatever; (2) they are generally cheerful and glad to see me; (3) they do not talk about themselves constantly or bore me with detailed stories abounding in such phrases as, "so I said to her, I said . . ."; (4) they can state an opinion or disagree with one without being quarrelsome about it; (5) they do not feel abused if I am not constantly available.

The opposites, those who make me want to run the other way are: (1) interested in very little outside their own lives; (2) make no attempt to hide their low feelings; (3) immediately begin to tell me how terrible life is and how neglected they are, usually with conversations reported verbatim as well as their feelings at every point described in detail; (4) are often offended at the slightest hint of reservation or disagreement—as a matter of fact, they not only demand absolute confirmation of their every utterance but want applause too; greet me with, "Well, you finally found time for me," or, "I've been *calling* you and you haven't been home."

119

The conclusion I came to—for my own life, primarily—is that to be eligible for friendship, and so avoid loneliness, I must be able to be happy *on my own.* That's why I said that this would sound contradictory. You have to be interested enough in something outside your own life to be happy doing it in order to be appealing to others. Just longing for people about you so you won't be lonely is self-defeating. People are never attracted to emptiness. If you are depressed because you don't have friends and you are not willing to do something on your own to make life more satisfying to you, you'll just have to be depressed. Friendships don't come because you need them but because you have something to offer in a relationship. If, on the other hand, you're willing to try to develop an interest outside your own life, to try to be cheerful and positive about yourself and your situation, then you have a good chance of developing friendships. Loneliness, that emptiness of life which surrounds one, is often the counterpart to an inner emptiness, and when that vacuum is filled, the other emptiness goes too.

TALK TO GOD

As to fear of the future, I know all about that. Every time my husband leaves the house there's the temptation to be afraid he'll have an accident (though he's a very competent driver). Every time the news on the 11:00 television news report is grim there's the temptation to envision even more depressing developments.

120

Ghosts in the House

This fear of the future—either the immediate future or more distant horizons—is so nebulous it's hard to cope with. The trouble is that the fear is of nothing real. Loneliness is real, sorrow is real, unhappiness is real, but what may happen tomorrow or next month exists only in the imagination. The only way to cope with it, therefore, is by pushing it out with something that *is* real. Prayer is real and is my first resort. I pray about whatever my particular anxiety of the moment is. Quite often my prayer begins with, "Father, I know how foolish this fear is, but here it is—please quiet my fearful heart . . ." and then I turn whatever is troubling me over to God.

That is the beginning. Next it is necessary to pay attention to something that has reality or the fear will come rushing back, so I get to work on whatever needs to be done—anything from cleaning the house to answering my mail or paying bills. I said that once to a deeply fearful young woman, and she said, "Oh, well, if you mean *doing* something, meaningless activity won't help. I'm looking for *answers*."

"What do you mean, answers?"

"You know, some meaning to life—something more than the usual Christian clichés. How do I know God isn't going to let some awful catastrophe hit me any day?" And with a few more statements like that she dismissed any thought of taking action to drive out her fears. She wanted to reason them away, and that's never going to work because they're unreasonable in the first place. The pattern the Bible gives us is always

121

a firm trust in God coupled with sensible, sound behavior. Both are necessary.

After reading as many of my own experiences as I've related, you may exclaim: "Good heavens, this woman has had every problem in the book! Depressed and hostile, depressed and afraid, depressed because of self-doubt—she's been a total mess!" The answer would be, quite right. And if I could find my way out of the morass of anxieties and fears and depression that held me captive, so can anyone. Not alone, of course, not in one's own strength. I had all the help I could use from the only one who can perfectly help—God. But not until I asked for it.

The first step, therefore, is to turn to God and admit one's fears and anxieties—however irrational they may be. There are clouds of nebulous anxieties which we don't dare confide to anyone, mostly because in our more objective moments they look so foolish we're afraid of being thought silly or neurotic. Just because one has a few neurotic fears doesn't mean the total absence of balance, and it's natural, unless we're caught in a particularly low frame of mind, to conceal what we're a little ashamed of.

You can say *anything* to God, however. In fact, it's stupid not to because He knows the secret thoughts of our hearts anyway; we conceal nothing from Him when we avoid the sensitive area and pray in generalized terms—we only deprive ourselves of the help He can give and which we need so desperately. Even when we find ourselves unable to express what we really feel so deeply, when the complexity and depth of our tangled emotions is too much for words, we can still pray in the certainty that what we cannot express He understands. Paul, speaking of this very matter, wrote to the troubled Christian church at Rome, "For example, we do not know how to pray worthily as sons of God, but his Spirit within us is actually praying for us in those agonizing longings which never find words. And God who knows the heart's secrets understands, of course, the Spirit's intention as he prays for those who love God." The Spirit he is speaking of is the Holy Spirit, the third person of the Trinity and the one who works in us and through us to accomplish God's purposes.

Once having admitted one's fear of rejection or failure or the future, we can be certain that help is on the way. To know that the God who created all that is, who sustains life and who cared enough for silly, blundering human beings to send His Son into the world to become one of them, who cares enough to listen to one timid, anxious, insignificant person praying is to know, at last, complete and unconditional acceptance. God has demonstrated His love for us by showing us, in Jesus Christ, what He is like in human flesh; He continues to demonstrate His love in the Christian community, however faulty it is; and in His people, imperfect though we all are.

KEEP GOING

Once one has admitted one's fears to God the way is cleared for help to come, and this is accomplished by several means. First of all, it is necessary to accept the responsibility for one's state. The mistakes parents made, conditions beyond one's control, the misdeeds of other people all may be involved and contributory, but whatever their influence each person is finally responsible for his own condition.

Again it must be said that we have the power to choose, and that includes how we respond to the circumstances of our lives. There is never a situation where it is possible to respond only one way; there are always alternatives and some of us must accept responsibility for the fact that we have always chosen badly. A girl I knew years ago was a small, tight bundle of anxieties. She worried about tests at school and got fever blisters. She fretted over plans for a party, prophesying all sorts of disasters which never came about. She was afraid of cars, afraid of catching cold, afraid of saying the wrong thing, and she always acted in response to these fears. No amount of encouragement was enough to try anything new from roller skating to meeting a new friend.

The change in her life began when she made a commitment to Christ and realized that to live in such constant fear of everything was not quite the style of life He advocated. I remember her very first attempt to break the old way of living. Our crowd had gone to a pleasure pier on the ocean front; one of those gaudy, seedy amusement parks of the thirties. We saw only the glamour, of course; the shabbiness is seen mostly in retrospect. At any rate, my poor frightened mousy little friend agreed to go on the roller coaster, a thing none of us expected. I was a little dubious, having mental pictures of her collapsing in a lifeless heap at the beginning of the first dip. She got on with a set, rather pale face and she got off at the end of the ride even whiter. But there was a glint of satisfaction in her glance at me, and that was the beginning of a different way of life.

Looking back it seems like an insignificant little episode painted in too bright colors. After all, she might have accomplished the same ends by less dramatic means; taking the initiative in friendship or learning to drive a car. But that ride on the roller coaster came at a time in her life when she knew she had to break the habit of living in fear. Sometimes the decision one makes may seem to be irrelevant to one's life, but it is significant because it sets a new direction. When the choice is offered, there is no waiting for a more advantageous time. The important thing is not how great a matter is being decided, but that one choose rightly.

The second step in getting rid of fearfulness and its depression is that once a choice is made there must be no looking back—no introspection, no wondering if it would have been better the other way. One won't always choose wisely or be successful, and the failures along the way have to be pushed aside and forgotten along with the alternatives one chose not to take. The important thing is to keep going on.

Just as giving in to fear makes one more and more

afraid of more and more things, so acting *in spite of it* reverses the process. Each time one gets through a difficult time there is a little bit of added confidence.

In the long run, the big decisions that change the course of a life radically are not made in one momentous plunge; they are the fruit of years and years of making choices. So in a very real sense there are no unimportant choices. Every time we decide for anything it's vital that we make the choice that most closely approximates genuine goodness; out of this small decision a life style is being created which will be as good as the sum of our choices.

CHAPTER NINE

Don't Look, It May Go Away

There are a lot of people in a blue funk because of their inability to accept reality. Every time the facts of life force themselves on these emotional ostriches the result is a case of the blues. It wouldn't do to be too harsh in judging anyone in such a predicament, however, since nearly all of us share these feelings at some time.

One might wonder why, in the midst of a culture that provides us more physical comfort and technical advantages—not to mention access to music and art and travel—than other generations dreamed of, so many of us find reality just too difficult to accept. I think the very sophistication of our society and culture is part of the problem. We have achieved so much that we are prone to believe we can banish everything that makes life less than perfect. When the circumstances of life demonstrate the fact that life still has unsolvable problems, we recoil with somewhat the disbelief of a girl finding out where babies come from. The real facts are so much less palatable than the fairy tale we've been brought up to believe. We discussed this attitude in Chapter Seven, but we need to consider its implications more fully.

It seems to me that Christian men and women—but especially women—face some very specific and very prevalent attitudes toward life that are at odds with our faith. We must deal with them, and we must face the fact that they exist in order to do so.

BEYOND OUR CONTROL

First comes the prevailing point of view that forces beyond the control of individuals are responsible for what we are. Whether that idea is expressed specifically or not, it lies underneath much of the thinking of our day; or perhaps it would be better to say it is in the spiritual climate around us, pervading the attitudes of people as smog pervades our atmosphere.

It's dangerous to generalize or oversimplify, but I suppose that in a way this wholesale abandonment of responsibility for the morals and ethics of individuals to society, or one's background or whatever, is one result of the belief that we can make the world perfect. Where there are problems, we tend to say, "You see— if everything were as it should be, I wouldn't be this way; the trouble, therefore, lies in the mistakes my parents made. I am merely the innocent victim of forces beyond my control."

While the Bible is clear about the fact that we are, to some extent, products of heredity and background (the sins of the fathers shall be visited upon the children even to the third and fourth generation), it also makes it quite plain that whatever a man's handicaps or advantages in life are he is responsible for his own decisions. Paul, writing to Christians in Rome, in his opening statements about man's responsibility for his own predicaments, reminded them of this principle. The Jews, he said, had had the advantages of the Law and of a special relationship to God; the gentiles had neither of these. Yet, said Paul, both Jew and gentile are responsible to God for decisions they make, for every man has a conscience which either condemns or excuses his actions.

Since the cultural climate in which we live is permeated by the assumption that whatever happens to be wrong with a man is probably someone else's fault, it inevitably creeps into the thinking of Christians. In spite of passages like the one just quoted; in spite of all both Old and New Testaments have to say about each man's responsibility for his own actions, we tend to drift into the attitudes of the world around us.

THE DEVIL VS. THE HOLY SPIRIT

One form this attitude takes, when it crops up within the Church, is that of superspirituality. In its most extreme form it is the belief that when one is rightly related to Jesus Christ the Holy Spirit acts in one's life so that there is continual victory over sin. Lapses from perfection are seen as examples of what happens when one gets out of fellowship with Christ; the devil gets in his dirty work and the believer sins.

Now I don't want to convey the idea that I do not

129

believe in the devil or in his activities in this world. I do. He is at the bottom, so to speak, of all our troubles. But the idea, at first so very spiritual, that what we do and what we decide is either the work of the Holy Spirit or of the devil is a one-dimensional truth; it's only part of the story. Being filled with the Holy Spirit does not mean that He occupies the space our brains once did. We are still thinking, deciding, feeling, human beings. There is an added dimension when Christ comes into our lives. We realize when we are honest that any goodness, any power in our lives is not self-generated but comes from outside. That is the Holy Spirit's work—to give us a new dimension of life. But we still think, we still act, we still decide. *We* do. Conversely, when we sin, as we all do, the sin is ours. We are not helpless pawns, sometimes moved by the Spirit of God and sometimes moved by the devil. To acknowledge both these spiritual forces is not to abdicate from all responsibility. The trouble with many Christians is that the truth laid out in the Bible—that the Holy Spirit is operative in Christians, and that the devil is certainly ever present to tempt and deceive— has been stretched into an excuse for everything they do.

It sounds so fine, so noble, to say when complimented, "Oh—it wasn't me—it was the Holy Spirit," but the other side of that kind of reasoning is that the responsibility for wrong acts and words and attitudes is handed on to the devil, an evasion of our own sin. If the Holy Spirit is responsible for all the good in me and the devil for all the bad, where is my own responsibility? We must all face the fact that while the Holy Spirit is present to enable us to live the life of a Christian, he will not do it automatically. We still must consent, we must decide. And while we may be tempted by the devil and see him as the adversary behind every evil, we must answer for our response to temptation.

Too many Christians are a little bit under it all the time because they have not faced this reality of life. Faced with choices we must make, confronted with situations for which we feel inadequate, we look frantically for help from God. That is exactly what we ought to do. The trouble is, we expect help to come in the form of a sweeping and sudden removal of all our troubles, a miraculous and radical alteration of our own minds and hearts. In short, we order what God will not deliver, and so we miss the very genuine help he does give. We forget that the Bible shows us a picture of men and women growing in faith, and growth is a process, not an instantaneous achievement.

That lowering feeling of depression so common to those who have been disappointed in their expectation of the Christian life as an untroubled progression toward heaven disappears when the true state of affairs is accepted; namely, that we are promised help in our troubles, not the removal of them; reinforcement for our faith, not a life so smooth that faith is unnecessary; and eventual triumph, not an absence of struggle. We are promised help beyond our own strength, but not a help that makes our own thinking

131

and acting unnecessary. Paul, writing to the Philippians, expressed the balanced life of a Christian this way: "Work out the salvation that God has given you with a proper sense of awe and responsibility. For it is God who is at work within you, giving you the will and the power to achieve his purpose." It is interesting to observe that in all Paul's letters when he makes a statement about the power in us that comes from God he always follows it by detailed instructions on living the Christian life. Nothing automatic is promised.

Then there's the ailment that is most truly Western and American—rootlessness. It is indeed a harsh reality that most of us have an uneasy feeling that we don't *belong* any place. We were not, apparently, fitted by nature to be migratory creatures—we like our comfortable belongings around us, familiar faces, neighborhoods; we like the feeling of belonging.

"Ah!" a woman exclaimed when I expressed that opinion to her, "but what about the explorers? What about the Vikings, Columbus and Magellan, the first colonists, not to mention the men and women who came West in the 1800s?" My answer to that is that we all have an urge toward adventure as well as toward security, and in some the former is stronger. But those early adventurers all had one thing in common: They took their culture and their viewpoint on life with them. The Spanish explorers took along their priests, their commissions and charters and grants. They may have been looking for new lands, but they took as much of the old along with them as they could. The English who settled the colonies in America named

132

their towns and villages after places in England, built houses just like those they had left, and the mark of that heritage is still here. Furthermore, many of the early adventurers had a place to return to. They had homes, a place where they belonged; however far their voyages took them, there was always that familiar place to which they returned.

They also took with them their world view, whatever it was. Their political ideas, their religion, their opinions on art and music and literature went with them, as did their moral values. The new experiences may have modified these somewhat, but never obliterated them.

We, on the other hand, live in a time and in a culture (the United States *is* a unique culture) that has gone through a process of throwing out very nearly everything. So much has already been written about our changing mores that it need not be elaborated upon; but consider how devastating that upheaval has been on a society that now, as never before, creates rootless people.

There have always been traumas—political and religious and personal. But they were experienced by people living in fairly stable circumstances. Families were there, often several generations. The town or city was very much as it had been thirty or forty years. People believed the same things, cherished the same prejudices, clung to the same ideas. When one particular aspect of life went abruptly out of kilter, there was all the rest, going on the same way, to hold things together.

133

The very weight of tradition would tend to keep life on a fairly even keel. And though much is made of the fact that the United States is a young country without the long-established traditions of Europe, still we had our own. It didn't take our forefathers very long to establish their way of life in this new country.

But today families are far apart, children often living across the country from parents and relatives. Towns and cities change visibly almost from week to week, new high-rise apartment houses appearing where yesterday there was a meadow, freeways slicing across neighborhoods and changing the landscape overnight. Morals and ethics once accepted as unquestioningly as the law of gravity are suddenly not only questioned —but ignored. In short, everything that once gave stability and a sense of belonging to life is either altogether gone or greatly diminished.

Perhaps people got their sense of security from all the wrong sources—from family pride or an unthinking assumption of superiority because of background or heritage; but at least they had it when they needed it. Admittedly, we ought not to rely on these ephemeral things for our happiness and safety, but they served as a nice cushion; and without them one must be in touch with a more genuine source of strength or the strain of living in a rootless culture will be too much.

THE DEEPER REALITY

It is possible to face the reality of today's rootless way of life, even to live serenely in the midst of frantic and unreasoning change; but only if one is in touch with a deeper reality. That reality is found in Jesus Christ who is, we are assured, always the same, yesterday, today and forever. When we look at our own timidity in the face of change, our own discouragement at being adrift in such an unstable time we can begin to understand why the New Testament is so full of caution against settling down too happily in this world.

Everything we have counted on to give us security—our culture, our homes, our families, comfortable values and a group around us who share them—can be both a blessing and a danger. They give us strength and stability when the going is rough, but they can also tempt us to forget we are, as Christians, followers of Christ whose kingdom is *not* of this world. We have to live in it, and make our faith work in it, but the moment we begin to settle down too comfortably we are rudely shaken up and reminded that it can't be depended upon.

Perhaps some of us are depressed and unhappy because we've been counting too heavily on the very things Christ warned us would not last; and they haven't.

The temptation to equate the Christian faith with whatever cultural expression of it we grew up with is very strong; and when we find changes taking place even within the Church—the one place we hoped we could be safe from disturbance—it's frightening indeed. The only remedy is a firm reminder to ourselves that our real safety lies, not in our church services nor comfortable group of Christian friends, nor in our style of living, but only in Christ.

LEAVING YOUTH BEHIND

There is another major attitude toward life that is widely held in Western culture and is wholly non-Christian, not to mention unrealistic. It is the idea that to be young is the highest state of mankind, and growing old is a process that must be halted if happiness is to be realized. All the sociological reasons for this phenomenon have been so much written about as to make any further analysis unnecessary. What we are concerned with is how we, as Christians, can recognize it in the disguised form in which it pops up in the Church, and how we can be balanced enough to avoid being affected by a viewpoint that is all around us.

We cannot succumb to this philosophy without falling prey to a subtle kind of depression. If we allow the idea that growing older is disgraceful, as if one's age in itself were a moral condition, we must inevitably feel that in leaving our youth behind we are leaving all the best in life. When one sees in magazines and newspapers and on television a constant glorification of youth, when middle age is pictured as a wasteland of bigotry and muddle-headedness and absorption in materialism, one can feel guilty by association: These clods depicted so contemptuously are past youth; I am past youth and growing older every day; therefore I too am a clod. No wonder I'm blue.

136

Don't Look, It May Go Away

Being young or middle-aged or old indicates nothing about one's moral qualities. It's true that there are some obvious and often caricatured prejudices one can sink into with the passage of time. But there are also the prejudices and unformed attitudes of the young. Experience has made some people bigoted and suspicious instead of mature in their judgment, but the moral stance of youth is often just as arrogant and one-sided. They can make the great condemnatory generalizations they are so fond of because they haven't fought any battles yet and do not know how inevitable is their own failure.

I think there are two desirable attitudes we can make toward the adoration of youth in our culture. The first is to avoid taking up whatever war-cry the young are uttering at the moment in the hope that this will prove one is "with it." The second is to avoid letting one's own opinions and attitudes crystallize in opposition to the young Philistines. It would be easy to fall into either camp, but both can be deadly.

The only way, it seems to me, for any of us to make sure we don't give in to either of these attitudes is to be willing to examine our own standards and attitudes and opinions constantly. Besides, Christians are commanded to do this in the light of the scripture. We don't keep reading the Bible hoping to stumble across some hitherto unrevealed truth, something startling we never knew before: We read because it's so fatally easy for us to let the truths in the Bible become crusted over with secular ways of thinking. We have to keep checking our ideas, the ideas of our particular group, against what the Bible has to say. As we do that, we find enough assurance for living our own lives so that we needn't latch onto the current fads in thinking.

BE HAPPY IN YOUR AGE

The only way to be free of either envy or fear or worship of the young is to be happy where one is. This marvelous attitude was exemplified recently by Dr. Pauline Alderman, Professor Emeritus of Musicology at the School of Music, University of Southern California. At eighty she is still teaching and writing and has enough projects to last her until she is one hundred. At a concert in her honor, as she received the applause of her enthusiastic and affectionate admirers she went to the podium and said, "It's wonderful to be an old lady!"

It is so difficult to accept the inevitable process of aging with its mixture of blessings and burdens. Maturity and wisdom, certainly, are blessings; and while they are not automatically acquired with age, that is the fault of individuals, not of growing older. On the other hand, the decline of physical powers, the lines and sagginess and loss of vitality we all experience are burdens to be borne with whatever grace we can muster. This two-sidedness is almost an absolute in life— nothing we experience is ever quite free of flaws; it is as if God were saying to us, "I'm giving you some hints of perfection to come, but in order that you might not settle down and be content with less than my best, it will never be more than a hint."

138

Don't Look, It May Go Away

However, we do all seem to have a tendency to see things in one dimension, and we seem to have an aversion to accepting the plain evidence all around us— that we won't find perfect happiness or goodness in this life, though we are commanded as Christians to work with all our might to that end. Because we find it so hard to accept the double nature of reality—good and bad, pleasant and hurtful, grand and mean—we often take a one-sided view of things. Some of us like to sentimentalize the process we go through as we grow older, as if the process itself were conferring upon us some kind of moral superiority. I used to know a woman like that who prefaced all her remarks to younger people with the words, "When you've lived as long as I have, you'll know . . ." She was cordially disliked by those on the receiving end of such advice, of course.

Then there are others who feel that growing old is such a dreadful fate that God can't possibly mean them to go through it. Not that they expect to die young, just stay young, presumably to subside into the coffin at last with unlined cheeks and the figure of a twenty-year-old. These two opposing attitudes toward aging are counterparts to those we discussed earlier— that one's ideas and thinking must always be those of the young in order to be accepted, or on the other hand, that whatever attitudes one has aquired in life must be defended rigorously against any alteration by young, new thinkers.

The balance between both sets of ideas is the same —a constant renewal of one's commitment to Christ and a continual rechecking of one's thinking against the standard set forth in the Bible. Without this balance it is impossible to avoid times of deep depression. Against the harsh reality of the vicissitudes of time, the passing of youth and the fleeting moments of unclouded happiness we weigh the reality of God; the reliability we may place in His promises; and the certainty of our destination—and find the scales tipped way down on His side.

CHAPTER TEN

Is There a Magic Key?

It will never be possible to sum up in one little book all there is to say about the blues, or about that acute and serious form of the blues we call depression. The premise of this book is, however, that there is far more that we can do for ourselves in coping with our blue moods and occasional fits of depression than is popularly supposed. We have been led to believe that whatever is wrong with any of us can only be dealt with by a medical doctor or a psychologist, or possibly a minister.

The current popular view of human nature is, as we have observed earlier, that all of us are the product of our heredity, environment, experiences growing up—anything other than our own decisions. My conviction is that whatever heredity and environment have given us as equipment, and whatever experience has done to us, the final responsibility for what we are rests with each one of us. *We* decide. This is not according to the spirit of the age, which assigns responsibility to everyone or everything—society, capitalism, racism, materialism—the list is endless and includes all the villains of the piece; everyone but the one person who has the final say in what I do with my life—me. It is this contemporary notion—I am not responsible for myself but can blame all my misfortunes and misdeeds on others—that we must get rid of before we can handle any kind of depression successfully. You don't get rid of the blues by saying, "It wasn't me, it was him."

There are three factors involved in our handling our moods: First, God is concerned about us all and has shown that concern by entering into history in the person of Jesus Christ, who shares our human nature and understands our temptations and our human fallibility. It is not a distant and unapproachable deity to whom we pray, but, as Paul put it, "For we have no superhuman High Priest to whom our weaknesses are unintelligible—he himself has shared fully in all our experience of the temptation, except that he never sinned."

He has promised us not only ultimate happiness with Him when we commit our lives to Him, but help along the way. The New Testament is full of practical advice, not only as to what we must do for ourselves but what Jesus Christ is doing for us and in us.

The second is what we ourselves do. The individual, as we have said an infinite number of times, is responsible for what he thinks, says, does. We have to say it that stupendous number of times because we are so slow to grasp the truth, especially when everything in the poular press conveys the idea that someone else must always be responsible for our problems.

142

Is There a Magic Key?

Our third important source of help with life is the Christian community; and that consists of whatever Christian body of people each one of us is a part. We live in a family relationship as Christians, and the family has been given the charge of caring for its members. We are never really alone once we have accepted Christ; we are part of the body of Christ, and as such we must care for each other.

THE SOURCE OF THE PROBLEM

The moment you begin to expand a point or probe into any area of life you discover that it's tightly bound up with all the other aspects of life. They have to be considered together; but one must begin someplace, so in our summing up we'll begin with the source of the problem—ourselves. And we start by facing the fact that every one of us comes into the world unique and different; even twins are not identical in every way, however much they look alike. Some of us are more gifted than others; more intelligent, or better-natured or with a talent for music or drawing or mathematics —the list is endless. We do not have the same equipment when we come into the world. It's useless to bemoan the fact and say that it isn't fair. After all, we are not responsible for inherited qualities, only for what we do with them.

We do not all have the same advantages in life— environment does make a difference. It's no doubt easier to be a nice, cheerful person in pleasant surroundings with good-tempered people about all the

143

time than in dingy, drab neighborhoods or growing up amidst sour, bad-tempered or negative people.

Both heredity and environment modify physical and emotional health to some extent—that is obvious. There may be extreme cases where a person has been born of poor, stunted parents—both physically and emotionally—and brought up in deplorable circumstances, subjected to such depravity that normal standards of morality and decency are outside his experience. But that is very rare, and in a sense a hypothetical case, since such a person would never look at, much less buy, a book such as this. No, anyone reading this book has no doubt had a background and upbringing somewhere within the bounds of what we call "normal," though it may have been far from ideal.

Now, whatever advantages or disadvantages we may have had as we began life, circumstances have also had an effect on us. Some very fortunate turns of events have given some of us a flying start in life. Others have suffered overwhelming combinations of adverse happenings. We have to accept the fact that these three elements of life affect us all—heredity, environment and circumstances. We do not begin equal.

CHARACTER AND WHAT IT IS

Having said that, we have given them their due. They have given every one of us either a good send-off or a poor one. They may have made some of us financially easier than others, or better-tempered or healthier, but they alone do not determine whether we have character or not. And that is where we part company with the behaviorists and the determinists, who believe that whatever character a man has is handed to him at birth and then irresistibly confirmed by his environment.

Character is what a man is—his habits and traits and set of mind—and is the product partly of his heredity and environment but far more of his choices. The small, seemingly unimportant decisions we make day after day are making us what we will eventually be, full-blown. A man or woman from a morally deprived background making the first fumbling steps toward doing good may be a far stronger character than someone whose goodness is the result of easy circumstances and no temptation to evil.

You can see that what we call "character" is far from a static feature. We are constantly on the move, constantly becoming. Nothing is irrevocable. That is why the New Testament is full of instructions on how to live the Christian life. It assumes the two premises we have already mentioned—that some of us are better than others as we begin our relationship with Christ, and that we can make choices. The promise is that we are given a new kind of power, help from beyond ourselves, and that no matter how bad our past lives may have been they can be different: "Don't be under any illusion—neither the impure, the idolater or the adulterer; neither the effeminate, the pervert or the thief; neither the swindler, the drunkard, the foul-mouthed or the rapacious shall have any share in the kingdom of God. *And such men, remember, were some of you!* But you have cleansed yourselves from all that, you have been made whole in spirit, you have been justified in the name of the Lord Jesus and in the Spirit of our God."

At this point I can hear some offended reader exclaiming, "Why all this recital of human wickedness? That's not my problem, I've never done anything really bad. All I want to know is how to handle my terrible moods now that I'm a Christian!" He may feel a little like a person who asked for an aspirin and got a shot of penicillin.

YOU CAN CHANGE

My answer is that what we really need to know is whether or not it's possible, given a lifetime of bad habits (even if they were only of self-indulgence and procrastination), to change. And the answer is, "Yes." Whether you were merely a whiner, full of self-pity, have blue moods you can't control or have led a life so shabby that the memories leave you ashamed and depressed, you can change.

This doesn't mean, of course, that the change is automatic or easy or without pain. For some of us, it has meant an inward change of direction, imperceptible at first on the outside; for others, a radical departure from their life style. Some of us may need the help of professional counselors—a psychologist or psychiatrist. Some may not. But for both those who need professional help and those who don't, the crucial point in handling problems lies within ourselves. The best psychiatrist in the world can't do for you what you must do for yourself. *You* decide. He can help you see alternatives, what needs to be done. But he can't do it for you.

I am convinced that there are great numbers of people on psychiatrists' couches after years of treatment—still talking, still dredging up half-forgotten episodes, still analyzing because they will not decide to do what they must do in order to be well.

My responsibility, then, is to accept the fact that I must decide. I do this a hundred times a day from little things, like being civil when I'd rather be grumpy, to big things, like refusing to cheat on my income tax when I know there's no way it could be detected. I count on the fact that I'm not doing it alone: "No temptation has come your way that is too hard for flesh and blood to bear. But God can be trusted not to allow you to suffer any temptation beyond your powers of endurance. He will see to it that every temptation has a way out, so that it will never be impossible for you to bear it."

The Bible never talks as though we were to have an easy life, free of the problems and sorrows other people must face. We are promised help—divine help for our needs—but not a supernatural removal service which whisks away all possible temptations and distresses.

Among the distresses we will have from time to time is the inevitable fluctuation of our emotional barometer. For some of us the swing will be wider than others, and none of us need to expect an even emotional climate all the time. But most of us can avoid being pulled up and down by our moods.

We must understand exactly what the Bible says about what God will do for us. We discussed this in a preceding chapter, but it needs emphasis for there is a Christian counterpart to the secular idea that we are not responsible for what we are and do. Instead of blaming background or heredity or society's evils for all our problems, some Christians assign all responsibility for their actions to God. What is worse, they feel this is a mark or great spirituality instead of being an evasion of accountability. Nowhere does the New Testament imply that in committing our lives to Christ we are automatically made good, or have become robots.

In spite of the plain teaching of the New Testament, however, the belief that spirituality is to be equated with push-button goodness, all the proper emotions and attitudes popping out on demand, is constantly with us. It is the popular vulgarization of Christianity. Those who believe it must necessarily also believe that no Christian will be really depressed or have any negative feelings at all because these are incompatible with their mechanical piosity.

No wonder so many Christians are trying unsuccessfully to cope with their moods and ungovernable emotions without success; they are barred from the very help they ought to have because to admit their problems is to lay themselves open to the charge of being unspiritual. Instead of getting positive help from the Christian community they will) be slapped with little saccharine homilies and Bible verses quoted out of context.

GOD, THE BIBLE AND YOU

Instead of this shallow view of the Christian life the Bible paints a three-dimensional picture of life *including* its hazards. Just as becoming a Christian doesn't automatically insure against ever getting a broken leg or an overdrawn bank account, it doesn't mean we won't have to cope with our mental and emotional illnesses. We never have to go it alone—God is there, far more than we will ever realize, not to lift us supernaturally out of the trouble but to be with us in it and get us through it. Paul, whose letters are those of a man sometimes low spirited, troubled, whose faith was no cheap or facile evasion of reality, wrote, "we may be knocked down but we are never knocked out!"

The Church was meant to be a community of people living honestly before God and before each other —so free from the need to establish any spiritual credentials that they can turn to each other for help in their weaknesses and for strength in their temptations. We fail to be what Christ meant us to be when we set up artificial standards of spirituality for each other. Not only that, but we fail ourselves, for if we demand that others present the facade of perfection, we certainly must wear it ourselves. When troubles come, the facade is a double barrier—it keeps us from getting the help we need from each other or from God.

Now that I think of it, some of the Christian groups

149

I've been in not only had no help to offer me when I was depressed or when I had made a mess of things, but they were a prime cause of depression. When you're trying unsuccessfully to cope with life nothing is so disheartening as to be surrounded by glossy people with a perpetual simper of happiness on their faces. I remember a friend of mine coming away from an evening spent with just such a couple. She listened to their effusions on the joys of the Christian life, their glib little catchwords and jolly stories of effortless Christianity in growing depression and said to me later, "Eileen, they're not real! They're too untouched by life to be more than cardboard."

We can break down this phony and brittle image of Christianity by refusing to conform to it. One Presbyterian pastor, Jerry Kirk, said it superbly: "When I share my victories and successes I inhibit people; when I share my weaknesses and failures I liberate them." His church is demonstrating the vitality and growth that come about when Christians decide to be honest with each other and *together* work out their Christian faith in everyday living. God can do great things in and through his people. He can do nothing when they are pretending to be already so perfect that no help is needed. Again Paul, as he so often does, has the perfect comment: "Carry each other's burdens and so live out the law of Christ."

We will be greatly helped in this by reminding ourselves that Christ died, not to give us an easy life, but to make us His own, fit for eternity with Him. In His

150

own words, as well as those of Paul, we are commanded to put up with difficulties and stresses of life in a style suited to His kingdom and not to give up when the going is hard. This sounds like advice to people headed for the thick of the fray rather than a grandstand seat.

The more one reads the New Testament the more it becomes apparent that we are up against all sorts of enemies of the faith: the opposition of the world, the machinations of wicked men, as well as our own sins and weaknesses and follies and unbalanced lives. Depression is an inevitable result of living in such a world with such a heritage. We must cope with it just as we struggle with all the vicissitudes of life: by trusting not only the future but each day to God; by reinforcing ourselves through prayer and Bible reading; and most important of all by choosing to act rather than remain passive. And that means living in obedience to God. That's why the New Testament is so full of practical advice on living, as well as telling us what God does for us, like this: "Don't worry over anything whatever; tell God every detail of your needs in earnest and thankful prayer, and the peace of God, which transcends human understanding, will keep constant guard over your hearts and minds as they rest in Christ Jesus.

"Here is a last piece of advice. If you believe in goodness and if you value the approval of God, fix your minds on whatever is true and honorable and just and pure and lovely and praiseworthy."

151